ITALIAN WESTERN -VIOLENT IMAGE-SAVAGE SOUNDTRACK

ITALIAN WESTERN -VIOLENT IMAGE-SAVAGE SOUNDTRACK

By John Mansell

BearManor Media

2025

ITALIAN WESTERN -VIOLENT IMAGE-SAVAGE SOUNDTRACK

Published in the United States of America by:

BearManor Media

1317 Edgewater Dr. #110
Orlando, FL 32804

bearmanormedia.com

Printed in the United States.

Typesetting and layout by PKJ Passion Global

ISBN–979-8-88771-721-0

Contents.

Acknowledgements and Thanks.

To: My long suffering wife and family, Alessandro Allessandroni, Daniele De Gemini, Godwin Borg, Lionel Woodman, Stephen Smith, John (Music from the Movies) Williams, Jason Drury, Tom Betts, Susan Di Bona, Salvatore Sangiovanni, Fillipo De Masi, Jason Piccioni, Franco Micalizzi, Marco Werba, Peter Boom, Nora Orlandi, Carlo Bagnola, Micheal and Carol Jones, BEAT Records, CAM/Sugar, Cinevox Records, Hillside CD Production, Roberto Zamori, Hexachord Records, GDM music, Laurence Staig, Tony Williams, Sir Christopher Frayling, and mostly my thanks go to the composers who are sadly no longer with us who took time to speak to an obsessive Italian western soundtrack collector. Thank you all.

Foreword by composer Susan DiBona

Classic Western movie soundtracks: all of us have heard them in some form or other - at the movies, in reruns on TV, in commercials, or on the radio.

Who among us, of any age, wouldn't recognise that harmonica tune from **Once Upon a Time in the West** by Ennio Morricone, or the legendary theme from **The Magnificent Seven** by Elmer Bernstein? These iconic musical moments are woven into our cultural fabric in the western hemisphere.

These are musical themes that make us sit up and listen. They create memories, and they reawaken them as well. Origins of the musical style we all know, and love can be traced back to the 1850's. At that point, a recognisable Western style of music began to develop, reflecting the unique mix of peoples who converged in the southwestern United States. The region was a melting pot of Native Americans along with a diverse group of Africans and settlers of Celtic, Spanish, German, and Anglo-Saxon descent.

Young men travelled across the land to work as cattle herders and cowboys, bringing their traditional folk songs with them. They created poems and often rewrote lyrics to their traditional folk songs more fitting to their circumstances. Their songs became a mode of communication on long journeys or artful shouts to help herd their livestock (the so-called "holler"), or to tell wistful tales of the loves they had left behind in search of adventure - and a livelihood.

Their instruments were practical, portable for travels. Playing them was a skill they acquired informally; one passed from parent to child over generations and geographical borders. The most popular instruments of choice were the fiddle, the guitar, or the harmonica.

The cowboys and settlers roamed the swath of land containing Texas, Oklahoma, and Arizona. They encountered Mexican musicians who had begun to develop a distinct style of waltz and polka music as well: they had adapted the German influences of their neighbours with the use of small brass instruments and the accordion. Reels and jigs came to the Old West by way of the Appalachian fiddle style. These musical elements became intertwined as various groups interacted, giving birth to new varieties of popular music.

Later in the century, quintessential American composers such as the Texas-born Scott Joplin (son of labourers who sang well and also played the fiddle and banjo), popularized Ragtime (an African-American march like piano style which later influenced both jazz and Classical music by European composers such as Satie, Debussy, and Stravinsky), which is often heard being played on the saloon piano in Western films.

The singular multiculturalism that prevailed in the Old West became the very origin of the vast musical treasure trove of the Western Soundtrack as a distinct art form. It continues to enrich motion pictures and impart a profound dimension of grit and realism to the stories told on screen.

The strength of the Western Soundtrack is this: it gives staying power to the stories and images in the minds of audiences.

The UK film music critic John Mansell, in this wonderful volume, presents interviews with film composers, unexpected anecdotes, and new perspectives on this still-evolving genre of film music.

This book is not only for lovers of the Italian Western Soundtrack genre, but for all readers who are curious to take a deeper dive into what goes into making a film score.

Susan DiBona, 15th December 2024, Praia a Mare, Italy.

Introduction.

I was first introduced to the Italian western score by mistake. I was about thirteen years old in 1968, and had already decided I liked TV and Film music after seeing *Lawrence of Arabia* six years previous. I wandered into a record store that also rented out TV's and radios in the centre of town. I started to go through the soundtrack section which was at the rear of the shop and found an LP record *The Good The Bad and The Ugly,* music by Ennio Morricone. I had no idea who he was, and the film was an X certificate so had no chance of seeing it for a little while. I noticed that it was priced wrong, and was marked up the same as the budget records on the music for pleasure label. Without thinking I purchased it and went straight home to put it on my orange coloured Dancette record player. After the first listen I was stunned a little, I had been accustomed to John Barry, Max Steiner, and the odd TV theme or two, so this sound was a shock, but what a sound it was. After this I started to take an interest in releases by Ennio Morricone, adding his first two Dollar soundtracks to my small collection. A year or so later I was back in the same record shop where I had found *The Good The Bad and The Ugly*, to discover *Once Upon a Time in the West,* was sitting in the same rack and again priced incorrectly. it was the French import of the soundtrack that had a stunning cover, and I think the cover had something to do with me buying it. After this I was more actively looking for Ennio Morricone westerns and looking out for the films at the cinema. It was not long after this that I found a place in London called Soundtrack in Gt. Newport street. The selection there was superb thanks to Michael Jones who ran the shop, and later became a great friend. It was here that I discovered composers such as Stelvio Cipriani, Bruno Nicolai, Francesco De Masi, Nico Fidenco and so many more. The Italian western soundtrack and the films that is was taken from were and still are a genre of music and film that has stood the test of time, both having a huge influence upon the world of film and film music.

Chapter One.

BEGINNINGS.

The Italian or spaghetti western as it was so cruelly nicknamed by French critics, remains a popular genre of film. It has over the years never lost its appeal, despite its quirky plots, and violent scenarios it has more than any other genre of film continued to engage and thrill audiences all over the world. It inspired many producers and directors to start making movies, and to this day continues to influence and entertain. So before delving into the musical side of things, a short introduction to the genre itself might be helpful.

SWORD AND SANDAL TO SIX GUN AND HORSE.

The Italian or Spaghetti western came into being because of the Hollywood Biblical epic. The genre began its life because of events that stemmed directly from the demise of the epic film as produced by Hollywood. For several years Hollywood filmmakers had been travelling to the famed Cinecittà studios and using its facilities, plus employing thousands of extras for the mammoth productions which also gave employment to hundreds of camera crews, second unit directors and technicians.

As the decade of the sixties dawned, the cinema going publics taste for Biblical tales began to curtail, people were looking for something that was different and more exciting. Because of this Hollywood moguls decided that it was time to quit Cinecittà, and by pulling out of Rome they created mass unemployment within the Italian film industry. Italian filmmakers were at first furious and concerned about the future, but decided they had to think of ways that they could save their ailing film industry, or it could be disastrous for the countries already frail economy. Producers in Italy had noticed that a handful of German filmmakers were having some mild successes with westerns, the sauerkraut western as it was labelled, had become popular within the borders of western Europe. With productions such as **Winnetou** and spin off films like **The Last of the Mohicans** shot by East German studios on location in Croatia. If one takes a closer look at these productions, one will soon realise that they were a clone of the American made B western film. German westerns being black and white in their storylines and scenarios. By this I mean the good guys wore white and the bad guys were unshaven and invariably dressed in black. The plots for these productions were also very predictable and clichéd, containing more than their fair share of the Hollywood westerns established format.

After noticing these movies, a few adventurous Italian filmmakers decided to attempt making westerns themselves, they at first took the lead from the Germans, and infused a touch of Americana into initial forays into John Ford's domain, thus creating nothing more than imitations of the German movies, which as I have already stated were themselves clones of American films. Early examples of Italian made westerns included, **Un Dollaro Di Fifa** which was directed by Giorgio C. Simonelli and released in 1960. The film starred Ugo Tognazzi and Walter Chiari and was an early attempt at a comedy western, it had a musical score by composer Gianni Ferrio. Then came another vehicle for actor Tognazzi in the form of the comedy, *I Magnifici Tre* (1961) again directed by Simonelli and scored by Ferrio, who would also write the music for a third addition in the Italian western catalogue in 1963 **Gli Eroi Del West.**

Duello Nel Texas was also released in 1963 and although this is not considered as a true Spaghetti western it is an example of film that hinted of things to come. The score was by Ennio Morricone but did not include anything that could be considered as being original, Morricone staying with tried and tested methods, and even including a very Americanised sounding title song. It was not until 1964, that we heard anything that remotely resembled what an Italian score would sound like, there were a handful of key additions to the film genre in that year, *Massacro de Grande Canyon*, which was Sergio Corbucci's first western, *Bullets don't Argue, Buffalo Bill,* and *Minnesota Clay,* the latter being Corbucci's second entry into the western genre, all being based upon the Hollywood tried and tested formula. Then came *A Fistful of Dollars*, directed by Sergio Leone. It was this movie that would change the entire genre of the western and not just for films produced in Europe. The formula that Italian film makers had attempted to use on their western productions was not that successful at first, the plots watered down and resembling American western films, but as soon as Leone stepped into the arena things began to alter and become a little more interesting.

WHERE LIFE HAD NO VALUE AND DEATH SOMETIMES HAD A PRICE. THAT IS WHY BOUNTY HUNTERS APPEARED.

(from *For a Few Dollars More*).

Leone's style of direction and his story telling abilities were to totally change the way in which westerns were made in the future, his vision of western movies would not only pave the way for hundreds of other Italian made examples, but also would in time also influence non Italian made westerns that would follow. ***The Quick and the Dead, The Hunting Party, Hannie Caulder, 100 Rifles,*** and to a degree ***The Wild Bunch*** amongst them. The Italian made western would be the opposite to the Hollywood incarnation of the wild west that had depicted cowboys, the central character for example would not be the hero that we had normally seen standing up to injustice. But instead, the main character in an Italian western was an anti-hero, a loner that was a bounty hunter or a gunfighter who sold his expertise to the highest bidder, as in the man with no name in the Dollar films. But even then, the anti-hero did have some morals and at times stood on the side of the oppressed as in ***A Fistful of Dollars*** and ***Django***.

The Italian western also included several examples that were looked upon as being politically slanted, a handful of these stand out as some of the best examples of the genre. This sub-genre of films were invariably set in the period of the Mexican revolution, these "Zapata" westerns as they were dubbed sprang up within the main genre of the western that was being produced in Italy. This small but important collective of films would often introduce audiences to another kind of anti-hero or central character who was a mercenary. A figure never seen as the bad guy, but more like a soldier of fortune.

Mexico was a dangerous place during the days of revolution, as many of the movies would reflect via moments of violence aimed at ordinary people, and in scenes where government led troops would be massacred brutally. The movies often featured villainous characters who were backed by foreign powers such as Austria, France, or Germany, who had only one goal and that was to get a foothold in Mexico by whatever means possible. The scenario for many of these westerns very often included corrupt government officials who would be supported by the Europeans, who assisted the corrupt characters with arms, troops, training for their soldiers and more importantly money. They would support the officials and assist in the intimidation and persecution of the ordinary people; this foreign power would also take great delight in systematically annihilating most of the peasant population. Enter then the mercenary figure, who would themselves be of either European or American extraction. This character would then befriend one of the peasants who would normally be a ruffian or bandit, the foreigner then schools the peasant in the art of warfare, revolution and sabotage and after a few minor successes against the government, the peasant then takes on the status of a Simon Bolivar, or Pancho Villa, figure amongst his fellow Mexicans, who look to him for leadership and protection. The Mexican peasant or bandit has been elevated to the status of a freedom fighter and a saviour of the people. Instead of robbing banks to line his own pockets he robs the banks to give to the poor, in the same way we are told Robin Hood did in England centuries before. The mercenary has been successful and has gained status and gold out of his coaching of the peasant or bandit. This scenario is best seen in Sergio Corbucci's, *A Professional Gun*, but it is also present in *Quien Sabe?* or *A Bullet for the General* as it was titled outside of Italy. This formula was also present in films such as *Campanero's* and *Gui la Testa* Aka *A fistful of Dynamite*. Maybe it is a little different in two of the movies, as in these the foreigner does not exploit the Mexican for gold or payment as much, but instead uses him to get closer to their own personal goal, for example in *A Bullet for the General*, Ninio (Lou Castell) uses Chuncho (Gian Maria Volonte) to get close to the General of the revolutionary forces so that he can assassinate him. In *A fistful of Dynamite*, the Irish rebel and explosives expert who is on the side of the revolutionaries played by James Coburn, befriends the Mexican bandit played by Rod Steiger to free prisoners from the vaults of a bank. Steiger and his gang think that the vaults are filled with gold but instead find hundreds of imprisoned revolutionaries, and unknowingly set them free. After this escapade, the Steiger character is hailed a hero of the revolution, initially he is an unwilling candidate but soon warms to the idea.

Although not set in the Mexican revolution, this type of scenario or partnership is also seen within other examples of the spaghetti western genre, *Day of Anger*, being one of them, Frank Talby (Lee Van Cleef) takes the tramp under his wing teaching him the ways of the gunfighter, but this backfires on Talby when the downtrodden character played by Giuliano Gemma, becomes better than his teacher. In many examples of the Italian western directors would weave a political scenario into the narrative or at least hint at one. Director Sergio Sollima believed that his Cuchillo character in **The Big Gundown** and **Corri Uomo Corri** was representing less advanced or third world countries, eventually Cuchillo rebels against his so-called masters, after rich rancher Brokston (Walter Barnes) frames him accusing him of murder in **The Big Gundown.** The Brokston character standing for the capitalistic western world. Sollima firmly believed that developing countries would one day revolt against the affluent countries of the west, he put this notion into the scenarios of some of his movies but presented them in the guise of a violent all action western.

Like all genres of movies there are good examples, bad examples and downright ugly ones, but within the Italian western genre each film had something in common. They were different from anything that had gone before, and they all contained music scores that were as innovative and affecting as the films themselves. The music underlining the narrative and bringing a raw energy to the proceedings, creating moods and atmospheres, and adding higher levels of excitement to this new style of filmmaking, a style that was savage and violent, which required a very different kind of soundtrack.

Chapter Two.

SCORING A GENRE.

An important and highly integral component of the Italian western genre is the musical score, and it is the composers of these scores that I have spoken to in interview and over dinners or coffee in Rome and London, I now turn to. Hopefully, the responses and stories that I have recorded from these Maestros can help us understand better the workings behind the musical force that became, the spaghetti western soundtrack. The composers that I have included also worked in other genres of film, and their experiences when scoring these are also conveyed within these interviews. It's a sad fact that most of the composers I spoke with are now deceased, but arguably this makes these interviews even more important, because we will never see or hear their like again.

There can be no doubt about which composer is mostly associated with the Italian made western. Ennio Morricone was the pioneer who was responsible for creating the unusual but effective soundtracks that enhance the movies of Sergio Leone, and it is true to state that it was Sergio Leone's Dollar movies that most film fans and soundtrack collectors identify as being influential to them personally. The sound and the mechanics of how music in an Italian western works is laid down in Morricone's trio of Dollar scores, and it was this musical blueprint that other composers would follow when creating music for westerns in Italy. This is why a similar sound for the genre evolved, a soaring trumpet solo, a whistler, choir, and solo soprano voice on the soundtrack to a western movie becoming standard, but the music for this genre is anything but standard or ordinary. There were many other composers of note that used Morricone's initial ideas about how a western should be scored, but they then took these ideas building upon them, adding their own unique musical fingerprint as the films gained popularity. Thus, creating a plethora of film scores that were distinctive and quirky. A handful of these composers are included in the composer interview section of this book, because they too were responsible for the development of the sound and style that was often employed in westerns from Italy. A sound that at first was looked upon as unusual, but in later years would be applauded and even mimicked because it was so distinct and effective. On many occasions composers such as Gianni Ferrio, Piero Piccioni, and Stelvio Cipriani to name just three, created a sound that was all their own, and although it was part of the genre's music, there are obvious differences and oddities of orchestration and individual trademarks that separate them from the style that was initiated by Morricone.

Chapter Three.

BUILDING ON MORRICONE'S FOUNDATIONS. COMPOSER INTERVIEWS.

NICO FIDENCO.

Nico Fidenco was born in Rome, on January 24th, 1933, and was an Italian singer who gained considerable popularity from 1960 onwards, after the release of the film **What a Sky,** Italian title: **Su nel cielo,** directed by Francesco Maselli I Delfini. Self-taught in music, Fidenco did a few cover versions of film title songs for the Italian market, which were popular and even entered the hit parade in Italy. This interest in songs and music from cinema led him to become a prolific composer for motion pictures. This interview was conducted in 1991, sadly the composer passed away on the 18th of November 2022 in Rome.

Q: I understand you received no formal musical education, and you are self-taught?

"Yes, that is true, I simply learnt about music by listening to it. Also, I was helped by being close to, and with, musicians and other singers in various recording studios. I listened, watched, and took note. By doing this I was able to pick things up".

Why did you change direction in your musical career?

"When I was singing, I did a few cover versions of movie songs: Exodus, Moon River, Suzie Wong and What a Sky, for example. These recordings were very popular in Italy and my interest in movies grew out of this, so I decided to try and write some material myself. Cinema had always attracted me, even as a child, and to be a part of the cinema world was like a dream come true. I'm still learning now though. Last year I attended a course at Centro Sperimentale di Cinematografa in Rome. So, at the start of things, I was not really a composer, and I relied on giving my basic thoughts to arrangers and others to turn into soundtracks".

What was the first score for a movie that you participated in?

"It will not be a surprise when I tell you it was a Western, a Spanish Italian co-production entitled In the Shadow of the Colt. It was a very low budget film, and nothing like the films of Leone, I think it was like the American westerns rather than being an Italian western as we now know them, but nevertheless it was popular in Italy and Spain of course. Well, I don't think it got released anywhere else, so I'm glad it was popular in these two countries, (laughs) the theme song became popular, and we recorded it onto a 45 rpm record and to my surprise, it sold over ten thousand copies in Italy, which at that time the early 1960's, was very good indeed. It was something that record and film companies would do after this, release the song from the movie as a single record, with a picture on the cover from the movie, the vocal on one side with a track from the soundtrack on the other. This way they would be getting more money back from the release of the film

because people would go and watch the movie and if they liked the song would buy the record, or later the LP record of the whole soundtrack".

At times you used the choir of Allessandro Alessandroni's Il Cantori Moderni on your soundtracks. What was it like working with Alessandroni?

"I never actually collaborated with him in the sense of writing anything together, but yes, I did have him, and his excellent choir perform on some of my scores. If I correctly remember John Il Bastardo Dynamite Jim and two of the Emmanuelle soundtracks were performed by them, and Ringo Il Texicano, I think. It was all such a long time ago, but Alessandroni is a wonderful person. He is a talented performer, with his guitar and whistle, and a gifted and very underrated composer. Nora Orlandi would also conduct her choir on some of my scores – things like El Che Guevara. She was also very good and wrote many film scores herself. Alessandroni was and still is a very good friend of Giacamo Dell Orso who conducted most of my soundtracks. His wife Edda has an exquisite voice and is responsible for a lot of work on Morricone soundtracks, as I'm sure you know. Giacamo would take my musical sketches and turn them into something special. He is a skilled orchestrator and an excellent conductor; I have to say if it were not for him my film music would not have sounded so good".

He also scored films himself, didn't he?

"Yes, he did a few. Two of his most well-known are for movies about Caligula or Roman times, which I think were looked upon as being a little risqué".

Were there any composers or soloists that the composer found interesting within the film music industry?

"Oh yes many. Henry Mancini, I think he was a big influence upon me. His music is so easy going and full of melody. Also, Dimitri Tiomkin, and Ennio Morricone. Morricone is an inspiration to us all".

Did you ever get asked to score a movie in the style of Morricone?

"Well of course yes, in fact always, everyone wanted Morricone to score their films, but this was not possible, so many directors would ask can you write in the style of Morricone for this film, well I tried, but Morricone was unique".

How long have you been associated with Giacamo dell Orso?

"It must have been forty years or more now, we still see each other and occasionally do musical things together, but I rarely write for cinema now and spend a lot of time performing recitals on piano in Italy and in South America".

Do you consider that the music you wrote for movies during the sixties and seventies has stood the test of time, and do you feel that the music that you wrote for Italian Westerns was good? I ask this because several Italian composers refuse to talk about their Italian western period.

"I cannot understand why they would not talk of this time, it was an exciting time I think, the films were being released daily it seemed and there was work for everyone, so I do look upon this period with some fondness. I do consider the music I provided for these movies to be good, and yes it still has a certain something to it now, but that is my opinion. I know that many Italian Westerns that I thought were great during the seventies are for me very hard to sit through now (laughs). Times change and so do tastes and styles. It's all down to the individual. But I think Italian westerns do still attract attention, and you only must look at some of the new movies and sometimes you can see Italian western influences".

Do you have a favourite score of your own?

"Yes, I would have to say Black Emmanuelle. I also consider that to be my best movie score, or at least my most memorable".

And a favourite western score?

"Difficult to say, as I did a few in a short period, Ringo the Texican, which was an Audie Murphy film, I wrote a lot of music for this, as there were many action scenes. But in The Shadow of the Colt is special because it was my first film".

What about a favourite that is by another composer?

"Well, I would have to say anything by Mancini. He is so good at creating lingering melodies. But there is a more dramatic side to him also, which we very rarely got to hear. His theme for Charade is incredible".

As a singer do you like to try and include a song on your soundtracks?

"Not always. Only when it is really called for, or if the director or producer asked for one, but no it's not something I go out of my way to do. Although there was always room for a song in a western, The Lanky Gunman from the Taste of Killing, for instance. If I thought the movie needed a song, I would suggest it".

Where do you get inspiration?

"That's a difficult question. Sometimes my inspiration comes from reading the script. Other times from a situation in the film, or even from a character in the story. It is different each time. Even at times one can be doing something removed from the movie, like sitting having a coffee or walking down the street and you get an idea, and must try and work it out, or remember it".

During the sixties and seventies many Italian composers wrote under aliases. Did you do this at any time?

"No, there was no need for this. I thought if I were not happy to write under my own name then I would not have written the music

in the first place. The music I wrote for films I was proud of, so I wanted my name on the credits. I know sometimes other composers used an alias, but this was mainly because the film was not good, or because the film company thought it would make the film more acceptable to non-Italian audiences in the cinema. But I thought this was wrong, so I always resisted using another name, unless the producers were insistent".

Do you have any thoughts about the way in which you are represented on compact disc? Is there enough of your music being released?

"No, never enough (laughs). Although recently a lot of my soundtracks have been coming out onto compact disc, so maybe more will follow".

And what of the future?

"I never look to the future. I live for today. Never look further than tomorrow and then we cannot be disappointed".

When I started to collect Italian soundtracks, I never thought for one moment that in later years I would be talking to the composers that created these quirky, innovative musical affairs, and I also never thought that the genre and its music would make such an impact upon cinema and the world of film music. I had always noticed one name on the western soundtracks that were released, and this was Alessandro Alessandroni. Finally, I got to meet him, interview him, and become friends with this underrated and highly talented Maestro. I sat down with the composer in London in the late eighties and we spoke about his career. His choir Il Cantori Moderni, has vocalised on scores for the Italian cinema that have been penned by the likes of Ennio Morricone, Bruno Nicolai, Carlo Rustichelli, Nico Fidenco, Francesco De Masi, Franco Micalizzi, Stelvio Cipriani, Piero Umiliani and Gianni Ferrio, to name a few. He is also responsible for a handful of scores for Italian productions and has been a featured soloist on many soundtracks. His whistle is unique and flawless, and his performances on guitar and sitar are second to none. It is Ennio Morricone that the composer Alessandroni worked with most extensively during the mid to late sixties and throughout the decades of the seventies and eighties. Alessandroni scored a new Italian produced comedy entitled **Trinty Goes East**, his music is everything that one would expect from the maestro and includes many of the stock sounds and musical trademarks that are associated with the spaghetti western film and soundtrack. The composer also shifted his location and was based in London where he hoped to raise his profile in the music fraternity. The composer died on March 26th, 2017.

ALESSANDRO ALESSANDRONI.

I began our interview by talking to the composer about a CD release which was a compilation of his works for film entitled **El Puro.**

"The compact disc is a collection of music from film scores that I have composed and a few tracks which are from soundtracks on

which I have performed. El Puro was a western, I wrote the score in a very similar style to that of A Fistful of Dollars, but the work on this score is all mine. The other pieces included on the collection are, Sinbad and the Caliph of Baghdad, La Spacconata, and a suite of music composed in the style of the Italian western. This is my own personal tribute to the genre and its musical sounds I have called it, Once Upon a Time-The Italian Western. On this track I have used the wonderful voice of Edda Dell Orso. The other cues include three tracks that were recorded at a concert in Salerno, these are A Fistful of Dollars, Death Rides a Horse, kill them all, and come back Alone. The latter being the work of Francesco De Masi who I have worked alongside many times and co-composed soundtracks with. The other two are of course Morricone. The qualities of the recordings are quite good considering that they are live. Also, Rossana is included; this is a very brief cue composed by Armando Trovajoli, which is just whistling and guitar. Finally, there is a track that is composed by Roberto Zamori entitled Stella Polare, this is also written in the style of the Italian western, and has a main part performed on electric guitar with whistling. Roberto is a music professor from Prato in Italy and is one of the people responsible to produce the compact disc, the other is my good friend and agent, Lionel Woodman of Hillside CD production in England".

Alessandro Alessandroni was born in Rome in 1925. He initially studied economics at university, and it was only because of his keen interest in music that he decided to become more involved with it and began to teach himself to play guitar and piano. Whilst playing in nightclubs in Europe he gained more experience and continued to pick up the rudimentary skills of composing and arranging whilst performing. After touring on the club circuit, the composer returned to his native Italy, and it was at this time that he met for the first time Nora Orlandi, for a short time he performed with her in a singing group called 2+2. After a while Alessandroni decided to part company with Orlandi and went on to form his own singing group which he called The Four Caravels, and it was this first vocal group that would be the foundation on which his now famous Il Cantori Moderni was built. Just after this Alessandroni received a call from Ennio Morricone, as the composer explained.

"I was in Rome doing a television show called Canzonissima. Morricone telephoned me and told me that he had been asked to compose the score for a western film which was directed by Sergio Leone, this turned out to be A Fistful of Dollars, Morricone asked me if I would play guitar on the soundtrack and also, he needed me to whistle as well; of course I said yes. Morricone suggested that the choir could be enlarged, so we added more vocalists making the choir twelve strong, and this is how Il Cantori Moderni was born. I am told that Nora Orlandi had originally been involved on the score with another composer, but I think that this might have been before Morricone was asked to compose the soundtrack. After this first collaboration with Morricone, I collaborated with him on many occasions and as you know on all types of movies, the choir was also expanded further after this and increased to sometimes sixteen members, depending on the requirements of the score".

Considering the number of scores that the composer has worked upon I asked if it was possible for him to identify one or two as being his favourites.

"This has got to be the million-dollar question; most difficult to answer. I think that I will have to say that the score that I like a lot is Seven Golden Men. I have very nice memories of this score and working with my very good friend Armando Trovajoli – I worked with Armando many, many times".

I could not believe how modest the composer was. He is after all the "Sound" of the Italian film score performance wise, especially the Italian western soundtrack and is the heart of the music for Italian cinema, but he makes no big thing of this achievement.

"I am a performer not a star, the stars are the composers such as Morricone, Nicolai, Bacalov, and others.

Working with Morricone so often I asked Alessandroni if he felt that he had been influenced by the composer at all?

"I think that all composers in Italy were influenced by Morricone. His output during the 1960s and 1970s was immense. It was also very good. I think that he also influenced composers outside of Italy and he created a sound for the western that is still being employed today by some composers. His musical presence was impossible to ignore."

Why did the composer stop working with Morricone, which is something that happened with others including Bruno Nicolai?

"I do not know really, I think it was at a time I was writing a lot of music for film myself, so maybe I became too busy. However there was a moment that happened when I was recording in Rome with Morricone on a score, which one I cannot recall, but it was a break in the session and I was practising a theme on my guitar for a film I was about to score, Morricone returned to the studio and heard the music and asked if he could use it on one of his scores, I explained it was for a film I was about to score. The Maestro, just said to me "So you compose for yourself now." To which I replied yes, he just walked away, and from then onwards the phone calls came less and less and I was not so involved on his soundtracks".

I went on to enquire about a score that Morricone had composed for **The Bible** directed by John Huston which was eventually rejected.

"I remember that Maestro Goffredo Petrassi had been asked to score the film first, but the director decided that he did not like the music so asked Morricone. Morricone at first felt uncomfortable about working on the film because Petrassi's music had been rejected, and Petrassi was Morricone's teacher and mentor. The producers of the movie kept Morricone waiting in Rome for a long time. I think that the director did not know what he wanted in the way of music and had asked more than one composer to write the score, and he was going to pick which one he thought to be the most suitable. In the end producer Dino De Laurentis decided that he

liked the work by a Japanese composer, and Morricone's score was not used. I felt disappointed for Morricone. His score was I think superior, and was easily his best work for the cinema, an exquisite soundtrack that was eventually re-arranged and used some twenty years later for a television film The Prince of the Desert. Morricone also composed some wonderful music for The Red Tent, and although most of his score remained in the film, the better cues were not used, it is such a pity because the best music was edited out. There is a sequence in the film where an ice wall falls into the sea, Morricone scored this with some beautiful music, but the producer decided to play the scene without any music, it was such a waste".

Because of his association with Morricone, Alessandroni must have met Bruno Nicolai, I asked him what it was like collaborating with him?

"Nicolai was a very competent conductor and a great composer in his own right. I collaborated with him on many occasions, even on an American movie, a western, the title of which I cannot remember (Landraiders -JM). I also worked on his scores for various westerns and some of the Mafia type movies that he scored. Nicolai deserved more recognition for his music, but he was overshadowed by the immense output of Morricone. I remember him being asked to compose in a style like Morricone by directors and producers because Morricone was not available to work on their film. Other soundtracks that I worked on with Nicolai included, Shanghai Joe, Indio Black, and Femmine Insatiable".

And what of conductor Nicole Samale, who was credited as conducting for Morricone on a few soundtracks after Morricone ceased to use Nicolai, or was this an alias for Morricone?

"No, Samale did exist, again another very fine conductor, but he worked on very few scores, after a short time Morricone began to conduct himself, what happened to Samale I cannot say, he just seemed to disappear. I think he went back to conducting classical music".

A score that was composed by both Nicolai and Morricone was ***A Professional Gun***. This was a Zapata Western which was a sub-genre of the Italian western, it starred Franco Nero and Tony Musante with Jack Palance in the role of the villain Curly. Alessandroni and his choir did a lot of work on this score, and it has many solo performances by Alessandroni both as a whistler and as a guitarist. It is surprising then that Alessandroni is not credited on the film or the soundtrack album. I asked him why this was?

"It is my own fault. I would often forget to ask for my name to be put on the credits. I was working on so many soundtracks at that time that I would not have time to finish one before starting on the next – there are a lot more soundtracks out there that I worked on and did not receive a credit. The recording sessions were often back-to-back some on the same day. On the soundtrack to A Fistful of Dollars I received a cheque for 50,000 Lire, this I think was about twenty-five of your pounds at the time, I only got the money because the record company RCA were so pleased with the record sales. Nothing to do with Morricone or the film company".

So, on *A Professional Gun* how much music was Morricone's and what cues were supplied by Nicolai?

"I have no idea, I was presented with the score when it was finished, Nicolai did conduct, but what music was his and what was Morricone's I cannot say – it will be revealed in years to come. The same can be said of Corri Uomo Corri, there were so many rumours that Morricone had composed the score, but it is clear by the orchestration that it is the work of Nicolai, I was at the sessions with Il Cantori Moderni, and I can tell you that Morricone conducted the score for Nicolai, this was because Nicolai was conducting another Morricone score in another studio the same day".

Wasn't the score for *A Fistful of Dollars* originally going to be composed by Angelo Francesco Lavagnino?

"Yes, I think so, but Leone changed his mind and decided to have Morricone instead".

The Good the Bad and the Ugly, must be the most familiar western theme ever written, and it was this that put the spaghetti western score and Morricone on the cinema going audience's radar. Alessandroni provided the shrieks, the choral accompaniment, some of the guitar solos and whistling on the soundtrack which included the now familiar Wah-Wah sound. I asked Alessandroni if he knew how Morricone arrived at the sound that he achieved on the soundtrack and why he decided to score it in this way?

"There were many stories circulating at the time about how the sound came about, some saying that the composer had based them on animal noises, others suggesting that Morricone had got the ideas by listening to Indian chants, but I can honestly say I do not know how they were conceived. All I know is that the work was all from Morricone".

When Alessandroni is asked to perform on a score, who decides what section of music will be whistled etc?

"Again, I cannot say for sure, when one collaborates with another composer, things just happen, it's a creative process that sometimes is a joint effort and other times is the work of just one person. With Morricone he orchestrated the scores and was clear about what sound he needed. I began whistling by accident – Maestro Nino Rota wanted a whistler for a soundtrack, and I volunteered, sometimes a performer can suggest something to a composer and the composer uses it, but it is in the end the decision of the composer".

And how did Alessandroni work out his musical ideas for a film score?

"Generally, I use a piano to try things out, but sometimes I will use guitar. I have more recently begun to use a computer but still I prefer to use real musical instruments. A computer or a synthesiser can sound bland and artificial at times. There is a time and place for this type of music, normally when time is short or the budget is very tight, or the movie is not so good".

Alessandroni Scored **Around the World with the Lovers of Peynet** after Ennio Morricone was unable to work on the movie, with just the theme for the movie being written by Ennio Morricone. I asked Alessandroni how he became involved on this score?

"Morricone was asked to do the score, and he accepted the project but found himself unable to fulfil the assignment due to working on other movies, so he composed a piece which was used as the films main theme and asked me to provide the remainder of the score. I did base some of my music on Morricone's theme but developed it further into other compositions. The theme that Morricone wrote was also used as the films love theme. I enjoyed working on this project – it was a full-length animated movie, and the soundtrack was issued in Japan on an LP, and then a little while ago it was re-issued on a double CD".

Like Alessandroni, Edda Dell Orso is an artist that has worked on many soundtracks and has worked with most Italian film music composers. I asked Alessandroni about her.

"Edda, I liked very much to work with; she never ceased to amaze me. I have collaborated with her on numerous occasions, and I have also collaborated with her husband Giacamo Dell Orso, who is a very underrated composer, and a very talented conductor and arranger. Edda, s voice is flawless, and she has such a range in her vocals. Without her, Italian film music would not have been so popular, I am certain".

My final question to Alessandroni was, are you working on anything now?

"As you know my last score was for Trinity Goes East, I have moved my studio to London. There was some interest from various people, and I have just finished filming a documentary for a British television company. I will also be performing in concert in London and there is also the possibility of another recording of my music being released by another British company; but now I am travelling and enjoying life".

For the next two interviews I was in Rome, it was October 4th, 2006. I was lucky enough to be invited to the offices of the well-known record label Beat. The temperatures were in the mid 80's and I decided to take a taxi from Vatican City to my destination which was just a little way from the impressive architecture of the Pope's residence. I was greeted warmly by Daniele De Gemini who very soon introduced me to the esteemed and respected musician Franco De Gemini. We went to Mr. De Gemini's office and sat for a while just chatting. After which he began to relay to me stories about recording sessions and about concerts and specific film scores on which he had worked.

I was amazed to find out that he had played harmonica on no less than eight hundred film scores. I remember thinking to myself, God I don't think I have or will ever see eight hundred movies in my lifetime. One story that stuck in my mind was about Ennio Morricone. De Gemini had been asked to play harmonica on a score by the maestro, but the score began with a very low bass note. De Gemini explained it was impossible for him to play this note first thing in the morning at this session, so he told Morricone that the note could not be played on the harmonica. The Maestro accepted his word and made the necessary alterations to the score.

Some weeks later De Gemini found himself in the studio again with Morricone and again the Maestro had begun his score with a very low bass note. De Gemini reminded the maestro that this note could not be played on the harmonica. Morricone looked at him and then produced a harmonica of his own, played the note and told Franco *"Once you can get away with it but twice NO"*. There was also a story that involved Leonard Bernstein, De Gemini played harmonica on West Side Story, he began to play at the recording session, and Bernstein called a halt to the recording, calling the harmonica player over to him mis-pronouncing his name as De Jeminy, he asked him why he was playing in the way he did. De Gemini shrugged his shoulders saying this is how I play. Bernstein produced a record of a harmonica player performing a piece of music. He played it for De Gemini, saying this is what I want. De Gemini said this person is a dog, I am the best, but the recording was of De Gemini that Bernstein had had for some time; Franco De Gemini did say I knew this but was not admitting it…

Mr. De Gemini also told me he was the only artist to be known for three notes; he looked at me and then hummed the opening three notes from **The Man with the Harmonica.'**

Franco De Gemini was born in Ferrara in the North of Italy; on the 10th of September 1928 he passed away on July 20th, 2013, in Rome.

Q: Did you come from a family background that was musical in any way?

"No. Not at all, my father was a police officer; my mother was my father's wife".

What musical education did you receive?

"My education was self-obtained; I taught myself and developed my own skills on the harmonica".

I was very young and used to play the harmonica everywhere, there was not much to do in my free time after World War II. OK let's say that there was not much time to waste in that period also. Nevertheless, my specialisation began in the 1950s and it was at this time I played on my first soundtrack".

Do you play any other instrument at all?

"No not at all, although I do play lots of different harmonicas".

Can you recall how many soundtracks or recordings on which you have performed?

"Yes, it is around eight hundred in all, maybe more, and that is just the soundtracks there are so many non-soundtrack recordings".

2006 was the 40th anniversary of the Beat record label, I asked the composer what was the first release on your label and what was Beat's best sellers?

"The first release was not a soundtrack as such, but a compilation of film music, Il Sogni Della Musica LPF 001. I do think that there were some 45rpm records released before this though. All the soundtracks of Ennio Morricone sell very well, but also Death in Venice was a best seller, and music by other composers such as De Masi, Trovajoli, Ortolani, Piccioni, and Piovani also do well".

At one time you had a Manchester address on your record releases. Was this your UK base and are there any items in the BEAT catalogue that were issued on LP that have not yet received a compact disc release?

"No, it was just a distributor that we used in Manchester. As for the soundtracks that have not yet been released onto compact disc. Yes, most certainly, dozens even hundreds, it's very difficult to say just how many, they will be released someday".

When you were working on **Once Upon a Time in the West**, did you have any idea just how successful the music and the movie were going to be. And did you imagine that it would still be popular so many decades later?

"Difficult to say really, I did not think about this at the time of the recording, I surely did my best in my performance to obtain a sound that was perfect for the movie. The film does bring back fond memories as does Italiani Breve A Gente, which had a score by Armando Trovajoli".

Your style of playing the harmonica is quite unique. Were you influenced by the performances of others at all and do you use a particular harmonica?

"No, I created that kind of sound alone; I consider myself my personal censor. I use a Honer Chromatic".

Because it is BEAT records 40th anniversary year, will you be issuing any more special soundtracks this year?

"We will release two compilations, this will be at the end of the year, one dedicated to Joe D'Amato, and one to BEAT and of course we are preparing the BEAT original book".

Have you ever performed in concert at all?

"Yes, many times, and still today I perform".

Can I ask what was Bruno Nicolai like to work with?

"He was a great Maestro; I collaborated with him on many scores including Allora il Treno".

You also worked on many of Francesco De Masi's scores.

"I played on around eighty percent of Francesco's scores, I collaborated with him many times".

What would you say is the most difficult score that you have had to work on?

"It was an American Maestro's work, there were twenty-five pages of dodecaphonic music, and I finished it in two and a half hours".

The next interview also took place in Rome on the same day at the home and studio of composer Franco Micalizzi, I left BEAT records and went in a taxi to Micalizzi's gated house on a hilltop in Rome.

FRANCO MICALIZZI.

Like so many composers that were starting out in Italy during the sixties and seventies, Franco Micalizzi began his film music career by scoring an Italian made western. The movie entitled **The Gunmen of the Ave Marie**, was basically a B movie, that received a very limited release outside of Italy, the score for the film was a joint effort between Micalizzi and fellow composer Roberto Pregadio, the style of the music in the score is very much like that of Ennio Morricone, and contains a distinctive theme which is everything that is now associated with the "Sound" of the Italian Western. Whistling, soaring trumpet solos, guitar passages, and choir all go to make up a very haunting and rousing opening for the score. This was the first thing that I spoke about with the composer.

"Gunmen of the Ave Marie was my initiation into film music, I composed the score with the help of my good friend Roberto Pregadio we scored the film in late 1969, and it got released in 1970, later I collaborated with him again on I Due Volti Della Padra and Lo Chiamavano Trinita. I must admit that we did write the score in a style that was like that of Morricone, but there again many Italian western soundtracks contained scores that were Morricone sound alike's. I am not sure if we were asked to do this, but it was done with the greatest respect for the Maestro; after all he was along with Sergio Leone the creator of the Italian Western sound. It was the hope of every producer and director in Italy to get Morricone to score their productions, but the great composer could only work on so many films, so the filmmakers tried to imitate Leone, and asked other composers to attempt to mimic Ennio Morricone, and this is what happened on Gunmen of the Ave Marie.

We even employed musicians and other performers that had worked with Morricone, to get the sound that we did. For example, Alessandro Alessandroni whistled on the score, and the trumpet solo was performed by Michele Lancerenza, both of whom had played on Morricone western scores, we also had the Il Cantori Moderni providing the vocals".

In the same year Micalizzi was offered the score for a comedy western entitled **Lo Chiamavano Trinita**-aka **They Call me Trinity**, the movie was really the first of its kind, as the mixture of spaghetti western and comedy had not been attempted before. The film was to be the first of many films that would star, Terence Hill and Bud Spencer, it was this score that attracted attention to Micalizzi from soundtrack collectors, the score not only serviced the movie extremely well, but it also stood on its own as entertaining music. It was a little surprising after the success of *They Call me Trinity* that Micalizzi did not return to score the films sequel, instead the task was allotted to Guido and Maurizio De Angelis. I asked the composer why this was?

"When the score for Trinity was completed and recorded there was unfortunately some misunderstanding about the publishing rights, this was between me and the film's producer Italo Zingarelli. This upset did sadly lessen our friendship, and I think that is why I was not asked to score the sequel. I am glad to say that this misunderstanding has thankfully now been cleared up, and our collaboration has now resumed which is better late than never as they say".

I continued with a question about *They Call me Trinity* asking how the composer got the assignment?

"The big composers at the time were not really interested in the film, the idea of comedy and the style of the Italian western being combined did not enthuse anyone, apart from the film's producers and myself, I think that many of the composers, Morricone included, were a little concerned that the film was going to turn

out to be an embarrassment to the genre. So, the producers decided to take a chance and offered me the score".

One of the highlights of the score is the tongue in cheek title song, I asked the composer about the song and who decided that the film required a vocal?

"It was a joint decision between the director, Enzo Barboni, the producer and myself. We discussed the possibility of a song on the titles, and it was decided that a vocal would attract more attention to the movie".

And why did the composer have the vocals sung in English?

"There was at that time in Italy an opinion that if American or English actors were in leading roles in Italian made westerns that the film would stand a better chance of success when and if it was released outside of Europe, and this opinion also applied to the music in films, so a song that was sung in English was thought to be much more advantageous to the film's success. I suppose that to a degree this was true, and the single 45rpm release of the Trinity song sold very well in Italy, and many copies were exported to America and England. A very good friend of mine in England Lally Stott wrote the lyrics, he understood perfectly what I wanted, and what I wanted to achieve. Sadly, Lally died a few years later in a boating accident in Liverpool, the song is a send up of all other western songs, as the film itself was a parody of other westerns, both American and Italian".

The composer enjoyed a little limelight during the 1970's outside of Italy, when he scored the romantically slanted tearjerker of a movie **The Last Snows of Spring**. Which did well at the box office, and Micalizzi, s music was also something of a hit. For this soundtrack, the composer employed a very rich and lush score, which again was very similar to the style of Ennio Morricone, selections from the film were released on RCA Original Cast in Italy and sold moderately well. With an edition of the soundtrack being on K-Tel records outside of Italy and even being advertised on television. Micalizzi followed this success with something in a similar vein. **The Tree with Pink Leaves** was also a weepy, and because of the films appeal a soundtrack album was issued in Italy on the Cinevox label. But apart from these two albums and the LP releases of **They Call me Trinity** and the second-rate Exorcist clone movie, **The Devil Within Her**, Micalizzi has been without representation as far as recordings of his scores are concerned. I asked the Maestro if he felt a little disappointed that his music for film was not easy to obtain on any type of recording?

"I do feel that maybe more of my film scores should have been released onto disc, in fact RCA did issue a Best of LP, which had various themes of mine on it, this however has not been re-issued onto CD as of yet, but soundtracks I think are not a big profit maker for the record companies, and outside of Italy I think that you would find it difficult to get any of my records, this is because many of the films that I worked upon, did not get a release outside of Italy, so people did not know about them. It is only people like yourself that know of their existence. Also, music publishers were

not interested in soundtracks, when they could deal with more profitable things, such as popular music".

Many composers released their music on their own recording labels, is this something that Micalizzi had thought about?

"No, not really, if I am totally honest, I don't think that I would sell many copies. Soundtracks have a very little market, and they are very expensive to produce. They are very complicated things to release, there are many things to consider, such as re-use payments, and it can become a nightmare in the end. It is better to leave such things to the larger companies such as RCA, CAM, and BEAT. Although the two western scores that we have spoken about Trinity and The Gunmen of the Ave have just been released on CD by an English recording company that has links with Italy, and Lucrezia Giovane got issued on BEAT, also my score for Stridulum has been released by RCA, but only in Italy. Over the past few years, I have been concentrating on writing music for the Ariola music library, this will in the end consist of some 60 CD, s. I am also in the process of producing a collection for my own company which is called The New Tea Dance Music Company".

Did the rights to his film scores belong to him?

"The music that I have written for the cinema is normally owned by the film company that has released the movie, or the music publisher who has financed the soundtrack. Again, this can vary from

project to project. But it is normally the music publishers that own the copyright on film soundtracks in Italy".

So, what made the composer decide that he wanted to write music for film?

"I had always had a big love for the cinema, and music was and is still important to me. So, I obviously took particular interest in the music in films. Cinema was a very important source of culture for people of my generation, I was fascinated by how the music worked with the film, and this is what made me decide that I would like to compose music for the cinema. The idea of doing this intrigued me immensely".

I continued by asking the composer if any of his family were musical at all?

"No, it was not a tradition in my family to be involved in music professionally, although I did show an interest in music from a very early age, I could only devote myself to study music privately, and this was at the end of my education at high school. I gained most of my musical knowledge by my own personal experience and by studying and listening to the works of other important musicians and composers".

Was he influenced by any composers at all?

"Of course, I have been influenced by all types of jazz, and the romantic Russian composers, and finally I have been drawn from

the styles and techniques of my friends and colleagues such as, Ennio Morricone, Piero Piccioni and Armando Trovajoli. All of whom have been great points of reference to me".

Had Micalizzi ever written a score under an alias?

"No, I did not, but I know that this was something that other composers did from time to time in Italy even Morricone. There were various reasons for this, the most common I think being that the composer was not happy with his work on the movie. I always signed my film scores with my own name, even if I thought that they were not so good".

The composer collaborated with several soloists on scores for the cinema, I asked him what it was like collaborating with people such as Edda Dell Orso and Alessandroni?

"Edda is an extraordinary talent, to collaborate with her is wonderful, her voice and her great talent are unique in creating a sensual and lyrical atmosphere. Alessandroni, is a great talent also, he is so versatile, flawless whistling, precise guitar playing and a choir that is second to none".

Micalizzi seemed to excel at composing romantic music for the cinema. I asked him if he was more at home writing for any genre of film?

"The beauty of writing for the cinema is that you get the opportunity to work on all genres, one week you could be working on

a western, and the next a love story or a crime thriller etc., every genre has its own stimulating opportunity for a composer. I do not think that there is any particular type of film that I am more or less happy working on, the real problem is to find the correct solution for every film, the right idea for music on any film is always difficult to find, and this requires work, concentration and of course talent".

Did the composer think that orchestration is a vital part of the composition process, and does he orchestrate all his own music?

"It is a very important part of the composing cycle, and yes, I do conduct all the orchestrations for music that I have composed, I would never charge anyone with this refined work".

Did he also conduct his own music all the time or did he employ a conductor on occasion?

"I do at times employ a conductor, but I also conduct myself, this depends on the film or the budget on the project".

And how did he work out his musical ideas, on piano or did he use synthesisers at all?

"At one time I would work out my ideas on piano but now like so many other composers I sit by my computer, each age places the best instruments at a composers disposal, but since everybody knows that the only really important thing is the original idea it

does not really matter how you arrive at the end product. Without ideas, no number of computers or synthesisers can be useful".

A point that is spoken of on many occasions by film music composers, is the very tight deadlines for each project, I asked Franco Micalizzi what his feelings were on this subject?

"Here in Italy, a director or producer will tell the composer that he needs the music yesterday, and I am sure that it is the same in other countries, music is often the last thing that is considered, which is rather annoying because music at times can either make or break a certain scene in a movie, I have at times been given less than ten days to complete a score, and that is composing and actually scoring the movie, I am of the opinion that a composer should be given a lot more time than this, and also that a composer should be involved with a film as early as possible, right from the beginning with the script for example. This gives the composer a chance to find out what the film is about, and also get involved with the storyline, it gives him the opportunity to develop themes etc., for each of the characters in the film, and also music can also be played during the filming of certain scenes, which will obviously also help the actors and director create the correct atmosphere".

And what was his opinion of the use of a temp track on a film, did he think that this assisted the composer, or did it distract him?

"This I think is a pointless exercise, the use of a temp track is a most destructive thing to do to a composer".

And what of the future?

"As I have already said, I am busy recording a lot of music for various music libraries, and this is taking up a lot of my time, in Italy the cinema industry is having a tough time, this is because of the development of television, there are now so many channels, offering such a variety of films, documentaries etc, so people tend not to go to the cinema as much as they used too. This has damaged the film industry considerably and has effectively sunk the great Italian cinema. I hope that new laws may soon balance the further development of these forms of art and entertainment".

The third interview I conducted in Rome was with Maestro Stelvio Cipriani, which I did the following day. Cipriani like all the Italian Maestro's was gracious and genuinely interested in why I was interested in his music. Stelvio Cipriani was born on August 20th, 1937. He scored several Italian westerns, but worked prolifically scoring romantic movies, police and crime dramas, and horror films. He passed away on October 1st, 2018.

STELVIO CIPRIANI.

Q. Did you come from a family background that was musical at all?

"Nobody in my family was interested in music. I became involved with music accidentally: It was something innate inside me! I qualified and for one year I worked as accountant, but during this year I was also studying at the conservatory".

What musical education did you receive?

"When I was a child, I usually went to church, and I was fascinated by the organ. A priest gave me my first lessons: he taught me the ABC… the five-line stave… and he was the one who signalled my grandfather about my big improvements and great interest in music. Everybody in my family wondered who I was like! At fourteen I sat the exams to enter the conservatory… and from that time I have never stopped with music".

Had you always wanted to write music for the cinema, or was this something that developed as your career progressed and what was your first film score?

"My first movie was Bounty Killer, a western, it was July 10th, 1966: my film music career started with that movie. I could exploit that opportunity thanks to my previous experience, differently from the present composers… Experience is very important: after my training and experience in piano, before starting with soundtracks, I lived many different situations. I played for six months, with a small music band, on cruise ships. At that time there were many ballrooms (or "balere" in Italian) – it was a very popular fad! – and we played in the manner of many other bands… like Peppino Di Capri and Fred Bongusto, to tell only two names. These ships sailed from New York to Portorico, Haiti, and Caribbean Sea. When I came back to Italy, I was enlisted as pianist and accompanist by Rita Pavone the famous singer, who at the time started her career. Again, I'm never stopping to repeat how these experiences

were fundamental for my skill and proficiency. An essential plat-
form that after five years, would have given me a useful knowl-
edge, necessary to work in cinema".

Your style is very original and, in many ways, unique, do you under-take all the orchestration work on your scores for the cinema?

"Yes, I am personally interested in it. When you have the possibil-
ity to do it, I think it's important".

When you are working on a motion picture assignment, how many times do you like to watch a movie to get any ideas as to, what type of music is to be written or where the music should be placed for best effect?

"This is an interesting question. I think the answer is subjec-
tive for any composer. I certainly need to remember exactly
the images while I compose music, but fortunately I have an
impressing photographic memory! I don't need to see the movie
many times. Sometimes Dino Risi was impressed by my memory
because I remembered better than him any particulars of the
frames. I would at times make fun of him joking about our age
gap, saying he was getting old, and he could not remember the
movie".

You have toured with orchestras and given concerts of your film music and other composer's works, are there any composers that you find particularly interesting or original? Are there any composers that you think may have influenced you in the way that you compose or orchestrate your music?

"When I was young, I was a great fan of Henry Mancini… and still I am! He represented an aim for me, like a searchlight in the sea. While I was working at my second movie, Un Uomo, Un Cavallo, Una Pistola, I was very honoured because his attention to my music theme from the film. I don't know… it's a very big satisfaction: it's a sign of your artistic value! When a few years later I met him, he was amazed to know me in person and said: – I thought you were older, with white hair! I studied on his books; I still have them. I did not imitate him, but I considered him as an example by a professional point of view. As for Italian composers, the great Nino Rota would have to be the top of my list, he became very famous thanks to his soundtracks in Fellini's movies, and he was a very complete musician. I often play Italian composer's themes in my concerts ("Via col vento", "Il padrino", "L'amore è una cosa meravigliosa", ma anche "Titanic"!) and I usually start with Nino Rota's music this is out of, respect for his wonderful talent… then, in the end, I conclude with Anonimo Veneziano! Which of course is my own composition".

Your score for **Un Uomo Un Cavallo Una Pistola,** is now famous and considered a classic, the theme is one of the Italian western genres most popular musical works. How did you become involved with this project, and what size orchestra did you use on the score?

"It was because of the work I had done previously on The Bounty Hunter, the director wanted me, so he contacted me, and I agreed

to write the score. I would say the size of the orchestra was number to between thirty and thirty five players".

You have worked with both Alessandroni and Nora Orlandi's choirs. Did you have a preference to which vocal group that you used, or was it just a matter of availability?

"No preferences. They're both very good and, moreover, they're great professionals. My choices were merely based on their availability".

Several of your film scores, have recently been issued for the first time on the Digit Movies Label, are you pleased that these are now finally available to collectors, and did you have any involvement in the preparation of the releases?

"Surely! It pleases me a lot! But I don't intervene… I leave them free to choose".

Have you ever composed a film score under another name?

"Yes I have, my nickname was Steve Powder, a "revisiting" to my real name: Stelvio became Steve, Cipriani became Powder, because in Italian it means the beauty face powder. I used it on a movie Piranha ll, which was not a great success".

What do you consider to be the role of music in film?

"It's undoubtedly fundamental, it's an integral part in a movie… but of course a good soundtrack is more enhanced when the movie is good too".

How much time were you normally given to compose a score for a movie, maybe you would like to use **L, Iguana Dalla Lingua Di Fuoco** as an example?

"One month, normally, considering all the movie's phases: to watch the film, to compose the music, to orchestrate and record it".

When working on a film score, how do arrive at your musical solutions, do you use piano, synthesiser or do you write your music straight to manuscript and do you have asset routine when scoring a movie, as in major themes first etc?

"I usually take some notes about the pictures, during the movie spotting session. Then, at the piano, I think again to the movie scenes, and I invent the music. I have a great visual memory, and I exploit it a lot to compose soundtracks. As for any set routine, well I, I primarily work to the key scenes in the movie, then, according with the director, I start working to the theme. When the director gives me his assent about the theme, I go on with the remaining scenes, trying to respect and to express in the best way their sensibility and feeling".

You have worked on numerous movies and many differing storylines and genres, is there any genre that you are happier working on?

"Yes... I have a deep disposition in love movies, classic movies in which I can better express my piano. I'm a hardened Schopenian! I love Romantics! However, I love to experiment new solutions too, relative to different genres... you must be versatile in my work. Besides, I like Italian Comedies, like Dino Risi's. Sometimes, thinking to my past compositions, I remember some strange contrasts... metallic music by one side, the Opus Dei by the other".

You worked with Dave Brubeck at times, what was your involvement with him?

"I met Dave Brubeck in a very emotional situation! I was in New York: when I was young, I experienced for a long time on cruise boats and those was the reason of my American stay. At the end of every cruise, they had to clean and control the ship, so we had a 3-4 day break. During one of those breaks, I was with my band's drummer Fausto, we went in one of the more famous jazz night clubs of the place: the Birdland. As we entered the club, we could smell a typical smoke and alcohol odour... and we couldn't believe to our eyes: it was the Dave Brubeck Quartet who plays!!! I fainted. Then we came back again in the club... and I was honoured to play for him at the piano the second prelude by Bach... it was one of the strongest emotions I've ever had in my life".

Where do you get your inspiration?

"From the pictures on screen mainly or the scenarios, but it varies on each movie it's a mystery as to how I will work it out. I can even

get an idea when I am not thinking about the film, and must make a note of it, because ideas do evaporate quickly. Every time I am in front of something new and I am amazed".

You worked with Mario Bava on several films, what was he like to work with, did he have much involvement with where the music was to be placed etc?

"My collaborations with Mario Bava have always been very good. He was a very careful director: he was always present when we had to record. However, I have been on good terms with all my colleagues".

Anonymous Venetian, is one of your most lyrical and beautiful film scores, did you perform piano on this soundtrack?

"No... that was Arnaldo Graziosi: a big pianist, and a wonderful person. When he was charged with having killed his wife and they asked my opinion in an interview for the RAI, the Italian public television, I put in the recorder the disc of Anonimo Veneziano, and I said: – This is Arnaldo Graziosi. He has a rare sensitivity and politeness. He is a friend with I have a marvellous relationship. He unfairly spent fifteen years in prison: I have no doubt about his innocence".

What are you working on now?

"Now I'm working on a thrilling serial TV, who is going to be broadcast all over the world. It is being entitled "The five senses of

death" and is being composed from five movies. Moreover, now I am working for Pope Benedetto XVI: I am very religious. One time I met Pope Giovanni Paolo II in Torino: an immensely spiritual person. While he was walking, he had all round a special light, he didn't appear like an earthly being. I composed for him some music in honour of Don Bosco. Pope Wojtyla much loved Salesians".

FRANCESCO DE MASI.

Born in 1930 in Naples, Italy, Francesco De Masi studied composition at San Pietro a Maiella in Naples under the guidance of Achille Longo, who was also his uncle. De Masi got interested in film music when Longo was asked to compose a soundtrack for a film, and he asked De Masi to be his assistant. Although Francesco De Masi was a gifted and highly original composer, and scored more than two hundred motion pictures, the composer has never really received the recognition that he deserves outside of Italy. He has placed his unmistakable musical signature upon countless films and although his music for film is not as grandiose or as operatic as that of fellow Italian composers Ennio Morricone and Bruno Nicolai, it can enhance, support, and perfectly compliment the action on screen, without being overpowering or intrusive. De Masi died of cancer at the age of seventy five.

Q. I am told that it was whilst still studying that you first became involved with film music.

"Yes, I was still busy studying in Naples when I became very attracted to the idea of writing music for the cinema. My teacher

Achille Lango, who was also my uncle, was asked to compose the soundtrack for a film and asked me to go to Rome with him to function as his assistant. It was while I was assisting him on this project that I made up my mind to make a career out of writing for film. So, I left Naples and moved to Rome and in 1951 I scored my first film; this was not a feature but a documentary which was entitled Fiat Panis".

During the following seven years I think you worked on numerous documentaries.

"I remember one series of films. I went on location to Argentina for this and stayed there for about eight months or so with the crew and managed to collect documentation etc. on local music. This was very useful and assisted me a great deal when it came to composing the soundtrack. The film that I initially worked on for this series was entitled, Dagli Appennini Alle Ande, directed by Folco Quilici. All the films in the series were about Polynesia".

Like many composers in Italy during the '60s you were busy scoring westerns. You were responsible for many soundtracks for these sagebrush sagas. One earned you recognition outside of your native country. This was **Arizona Colt** which contained the theme song *The Man from Nowhere*.

"I composed the theme and some of the score for Arizona Colt with Alessandro Alessandroni. This was the first time that I had collaborated with him and thankfully this collaboration continued with

other film scores and developed into a great friendship. Collaborating with a musician such as Alessandro is always interesting and most certainly always stimulating".

How much time did you get to score westerns that were being produced at that time – taking *Arizona Colt* as an example?

"I can only say not long enough time. It is always the same when scoring pictures. The directors want the score ready before you have started and that is the same for each genre, not just westerns. I think that I took three weeks to complete the music for Arizona Colt, I would have liked longer, but it was not possible. The normal amount of time I used to be given was a month if I was lucky".

Record companies have been re-issuing several older soundtracks on compact disc. Do you think there is enough of your music available to collectors?

"There have been many records released and many that have been re-released but having written the music for two hundred and eleven feature films and hundreds of documentaries, I am sure that not all my works have been made available. There are several jazz scores that feature excellent soloists and there are some television scores that I think would also be of interest".

Many of your scores contain title songs. Was this something that you were keen to include, or did you receive instructions from the director or producers of certain movies to have a song on the score?

"I think that having a song on the soundtrack makes it easier for the music to be identified, especially the theme, and this is particularly true with westerns. If I felt the film needed a song I would suggest it to the director, or sometimes they would suggest it to me".

You have been involved with music for the cinema for many years and have worked on numerous movies. Are you more at home working on one genre of film?

"Let us say that I am allergic to stupid and vulgar films. I don't really have preferences for any genre. On the contrary, I think it's interesting to find, each time, the best solutions to any requirement arising from the different genres of film".

Your scores for the cinema are instantly recognizable. Do you orchestrate your own work all the time or have you used orchestrators or arrangers at times?

"I normally take care of the orchestration of my own scores. I am used to writing in a very big way, a complete score at first in rough version. Sometimes due to the lack of time I may use an orchestrator, but he must only do a final draft of all my indications on the rough version".

During your time within the film industry, you must have seen a lot of changes and many new composers appearing on the scene. What do you think of the new generation of film music composers working in Italy now?

"Excluding very few cases of well-prepared young composers, the line up of new composers that are working on films is a little distressing. Most of them lack a good technical knowledge and they are also lacking in the techniques of the actual scoring of motion pictures – these people are just improvising the job. They have little experience and have little or no imagination and lack the courage that is required to work on films. They are reluctant to experiment or try something new".

As well as your film music you are very interested in classical music. You teach at the Santa Cecilia Conservatory in Rome and are also the permanent conductor of the Conservatory's orchestra.

"I have recently been doing a tour of the United States with the orchestra from the Santa Cecilia Conservatory. We also performed in Canada. I acted as musical director for opera and symphonic music. I also compose chamber and symphonic music for concert hall performance and have recorded some of this on Edi-Pan records, which is a label that was founded by the late Bruno Nicolai and is now operated by his family. Some of my classical compositions have also been released on the Penta flowers label".

So, have you been influenced by any composers, in the way that you compose music?

"I think that anyone who says that they have not been influenced by the music of others, is obviously not being truthful, or they are a genius. I have been influenced by many composers, from Pal-

estrina to Stockhausen, everyone has stimulated me. I was always interested in the harmonic world of Ravel, in the theme construction of Shostakovich and the counterpoint of Hindemith. These I would say are the main influences for my symphonic music. My jazz influences would, I think, be the likes of Stan Kenton and later by all his followers of the California school. I must admit though, that the encounter that I had with the great composer of film scores, Angelo Francesco Lavagnino was a crucial part of my musical education, and a very important lesson in the actual technical aspects of scoring film. I studied with him at the Accademia Chigiana of Sienna and went on to be his assistant for several years. He taught me all the necessary elements of the job, from the initial setting to the development, all with absolute accuracy. Which is the only way to obtain good results".

And do you still write music for the cinema?

"I do, but only if the film is good, or the conditions are correct. It must be this way for me to be able to produce a score that is good for the production. By this I mean that I am not interested in working with inadequate means, such as keyboards, synthesizers, computers and so on, unless of course they are being used as part of a real orchestra".

What is your opinion of synthesizers?

"I believe music should come from within and not produced by artificial means. So, this is why I do not really like electronic

devices. The sound that is created by a full orchestra is the best way to hear music. Likewise, I never use a keyboard to put together my musical ideas; I prefer to imagine the music without any sound suggestion".

Have you ever written under a pseudonym for any film score and have you ever refused a project for any reason?

"In unpleasant situations, I always refused to be compromised. For example, the films that were typical of the seventies based on strip-tease shows and various vulgar situations. I turned them down. Unfortunately, due to publishing agreements I could not prevent some films being scored with my pre-existing music. In some cases, I would insist that my name be changed to Frank Mason".

You said you have recently been touring America and Canada giving concerts of classical music. Have you ever considered giving concerts of your film music?

"I have given some concerts in Italy where I have included in the programme some of my music from films, but I have never given a concert that is just film music. I am aware that other composers have performed some of my compositions within a programme of a concert that they are giving. I think in Sorrento, a concert is held regularly, and my music for the cinema has been played at this".

Do you like to work in any order when scoring a film?

"Firstly, I think that it is very important for a composer to be involved with a film as early as possible. Better to have a script and work to this – it gives the composer an insight into what is happening and enables him to work out where music might be required. This happens very rarely. Most of the movies that I have scored I have begun during the principal photography stage, or even when the film is finished in its rough-cut condition. When I see a film for the first time it's quite an emotional experience. It's at this time that I receive most of my ideas and suggestions from the film's director or producer, which will later help me to realize the complete score. As to the order in which I score a project, I do try and write the main theme first, this assists me when writing the remainder of the soundtrack. I find that if I have the principal theme plus maybe a few other pieces that are for the film's main characters, I can then proceed with the remainder of the score. I go ahead in chronological order, so that the score follows the development of the film".

You have also conducted several scores for other composers and a few years ago, directed the music for **Making the Grade**, which had music composed by Basil Poledouris. How did you got involved with that project?

"The collaboration with Poledouris on this soundtrack came from the fact that the score was being recorded in Rome. Because of economics, it is much cheaper to record in Italy as opposed to having the score recorded in America. For some reason Basil was unable to conduct himself, I think because of employment laws, so the contractor, a good friend of mine called Donato Salone,

asked me to conduct the orchestra. I have very nice recollections of working with Basil, and I consider him to be an excellent composer".

PIERO UMILIANI.

Born Florence Italy, in 1926. The composer scored a handful of westerns, but it is his jazz styled music for which he will be best remembered. Composer musician Piero Umiliani had originally studied law, fully intending to make a career as a solicitor. His keen interest in music however was to distract him from this profession and led him to begin to play the piano. He had been teaching himself the instrument since he was a child and by the time he was 14yrs of age had become quite competent at performing. It was also during his childhood that Umiliani decided that it was jazz music that particularly attracted him. He studied with Vitto Frazzi and later graduated from The Luigi Cherubini Conservatory in Florence with degrees in counterpoint and fugue. During the fifties, Umiliani decided to change location and move to Rome, on arrival in the Italian Capital the aspiring composer set himself up as a pianist, arranger, and orchestra director. In the early part of 1958, Umiliani made his first recording, this was an LP record entitled **Dixieland in Naples**, which was released by RCA. Soon after the release of this recording, Umiliani was approached by film director, Mario Monicelli who asked if he would compose the score for a film entitled **I Soliti Ignoti**. The film was a comedy and the first motion picture in Italy to have a score that was completely jazz music. Umiliani's music was so successful that it led to other assignments, which included film scores and commissions for jazz compositions. Although it is looked upon as the composer's first cinematic encounter, Umiliani had in fact worked on a film some three years previous, as he recalled. "**I was studying in Florence, and I was asked to write a piece for a documentary called Il Pittori Del Domenica, this was produced and also directed by Paolo and Vittorio Taviani, the theme that I composed Piccola Suite-Americana Per 4 Anche was not relay that melodic, quite Avante Garde I think, but at this time I was still young and enjoyed experimenting**".

Many collectors of soundtracks associate Umiliani with scores for comedies, thrillers and films that fit into the category of being soft porn or sexploitation. Movies in all of these categories were produced in their abundance in Italy during the sixties thru to the mid-eigties. Umiliani's style and musical approach was very much suited to these types of films, his scores being mostly light in their construction and being influenced with jazz flavours, and it was probably due to this style or sound that was realised by the composer that the majority of his music is now being labelled as Exotica or Lounge music, and is also finding its way onto countless compilations that are easy listening. Umiliani has become a highly respected and widely known jazz musician and composer. His jazz efforts often outweighing and overshadowing his works for the cinema. The composer's love of jazz is very evident and often manifests itself within his music for film. On many occasions this jazz style forming the musical foundation for his motion picture scores. But it has sometimes been difficult for the composer to incorporate jazz into his work for film.

"It has always been something of a task to convince filmmakers that jazz could be the right style of music for their movie, I have always been fortunate enough to be able to collaborate with directors and producers that I have had a good working relationship with. But many times, they have asked me to create a grand more symphonic sound, when jazz music would have served the picture much better."

One piece of music that the composer is readily associated with is the quirky and offbeat and infectious composition *Mah, Na, Mah, Na*. The tune was originally released in1968 and has over the years been re-released on many occasions and has become something of a musical calling card for the composer.

"Mah, Na Mah, Na. is the most simple and elementary music that one could write, so maybe that is why people have found it so appealing over the past thirty years or so, the voice on the song is that of my good friend and fellow composer Alessandro Alessandroni. I have collaborated with him and his choir on many things; Sandro has a great talent but is not recognised as much as he should be."

Mah, Na, Mah, Na was given a new lease of life and achieved a high position in the British pop music charts in the eighties when Jim Henson's Muppets gave it an airing, re-introducing the peculiar sounding tune to a whole new generation of listeners. As a composer Umiliani is very much like the proverbial chameleon, adapting and changing his styles for each project, enhancing and gracing each movie with his music, and applying his own individual mark to every project. He has also worked with and had his compositions performed by great artistes like, Chet Baker, Helen Mirril and Gato Barbieri. The film music career of Piero Umiliani spanned some four decades, and during the composers later years he continued to compose for the cinema and write sophisticated and tasteful jazz, which was modern yet easily interpreted and understood, and above all listenable and entertaining. The Maestro passed away in Florence on February 16th, 2001, aged seventy five.

PIERO PICCIONI.

Piero Piccioni is a composer that I have always found interesting, and his ability to adapt to any genre of film is at times astounding, his use of jazz and symphonic styles is masterful, and the technique which he employed on Spaghetti westerns was original and exceptional.

Piccioni avoided most of the stock sounds that were utilized by his contemporaries. Thus, making his work for the genre even more original and innovative. For example, Piccioni did not employ the whistling or the shrieks that were heard in many of the spaghetti western scores, he more often than not relied on the conventional instruments of the orchestra, trumpet, strings and woodwind, and although his music is from the Italian school, it also is probably the most Americanized in its overall construction, sound and impact within the context of the movie.

My first question for the Maestro was about his approach to scoring a western. Where did he get his inspiration from when scoring a western?

"My inspiration for music in westerns came from composers such as Max Steiner and more than any other Dimitri Tiomkin, his scores for the Hollywood produced westerns are classics and highly regarded. Obviously, I did not copy his style directly, but hopefully emulated it, at the same time following my own compositive instinct".

Piero Piccioni was born in Torino Italy, on December 6th, 1921. He did take piano lessons, but as far as composition is concerned the composer is self-taught. I enquired if the Maestro had he always wanted to write music for the cinema?

"No, I really wanted to become involved with the composition of pure music. By this I mean jazz, film music came later".

What was the composer's first entry into writing for the cinema?

"My first feature film score came in 1950/1951. This was for a movie entitled Il Mondo le Condanna, which was a movie that was directed by Gianni Franciolini".

I asked Piccioni if he had been influenced at all by any composer or artist, in the way that he composed?

"Yes, most definitely, Dimitri Toimkin I have already mentioned, but I have drawn much from the works of Debussy and Honegger, plus there is the jazz side of things where Duke Ellington and Bill Holman figured quite largely".

A question that I liked to ask Italian composers is the issue of taking an alias to score a movie, had Piccioni ever changed his name for any movie score at all?

"Yes, quite a few times. I would at times take the names Piero Morgan or Peter Morgan, this was at times to make the credits on the movie look more American or at times the director asked me to do so, and sometimes if I personally felt that the movie was not that good after it was all finished, thankfully this has not happened to me a great deal".

Piero Piccioni has composed many film scores, these have been for films of varying genres, I enquired if the composer was happier working on westerns as opposed to crime thrillers etc?

"I do really prefer to work on films that have a modern setting, the romantic and mysterious variety are particularly appealing to my appetite, then I can write either a jazz or contemporary classical score, and maybe in certain circumstances I have been able to combine the two styles, which is quite interesting".

Had he ever declined an offer of a scoring assignment, or indeed had he ever had a score rejected?

"I have refused several films and other projects, mainly because the project was not a good one, I have had one score rejected, this was for a film called L'Uomo che Ride, which was based on a story by Victor Hugo, and directed by Sergio Corbucci. Corbucci told me that he liked the work that I had done for the movie, but the producer, who's name I forget and is no longer important, decided to have another composer write the score. I was young and inexperienced at the time, so I did not challenge his decision, I went onto score many more movies, and the producer went onto do other work, which was more fitting to his aptitude and position, cleaning toilets I think". (laughs).

Italian film music composers during the nineteen sixties and nineteen seventies would on many occasions work in what has been described as a family environment, by this I mean that they would work within each other's orchestras, performing, conducting or at times collaborating on composition. They would also use the same soloists, performers, and choirs. I asked Piccioni about this practice.

"Yes, that is correct, many composers collaborated with each other, this was particularly true during the period when the Italian western was popular. I do not think that I worked with as many as say Morricone or Trovajoli, but I did work with Allessandro Allessandroni a few times, but this was on television scores, his choir is very good indeed, and as a performer he himself is flawless".

During the early stages of his career, Piccioni worked on westerns such as **Minnesota Clay,** and **Sartana**. I asked the composer about the scoring schedules on films such as these, as the budgets must have been a little tight.

"I would normally be allowed ten to fourteen days to complete my work, but this depended on the individual movie or the attitude of the film's director and producer. It also depended on what type of music was needed, whether I needed to write for a special instrument or had to include choir etc., plus as you are aware, many directors leave the music until the last minute, so invariably, I was told that the music was needed Yesterday".

Going back to **Minnesota Clay**, how did the composer become involved on the movie?

"Basically, the director Sergio Corbucci asked me, the film was very good, but unfortunately it was released at the same time as A Fistful of Dollars, so it became overlooked and was not as successful as Leone's western".

Did the composer orchestrate his own film scores, or did he use an orchestrator?

"I must admit I do not always work on my own orchestrations; there is very often not sufficient time to do this, so I have an orchestrator or an arranger. Like I have already told you, directors always want the music yesterday, and it annoys me a little that the music is often the last thing that is considered on a movie. One of

my very first arrangers and orchestrators was Ennio Morricone; he was also incidentally the best I ever used".

And how did the composer work out his musical ideas?

"I use a piano, and then I record the themes that I have put together, then I start to develop these and transcribe them. But I do sometimes write them straight down onto the manuscript".

I also asked the composer if he had a favourite score for a film, either by himself or by another composer?

"There are two scores of my own that I like very much, C'Era Una Volta, which was called More than a Miracle outside of Italy, and directed by Francesco Rosi, this starred Sophia Loren and Omar Sharif. I also liked Light at the edge of the World this was directed by Kevin Billington who is British, the film starred Kirk Douglas and Yul Brynner".

Remaining with **The Light at the edge of the World**, which was a movie that had its screenplay based on the story by Jules Verne, the film was very heavily edited when it was released, and at times was so badly cut the storyline became fragmented and hard to follow. I asked the composer if he had experienced any problems on the movie?

"No, not at all, but I did see the film before it was so badly cut. I really enjoyed working on the film, and as I have said I regard it as

one of my best scores for the cinema. The director was very pleased with my work on his film, in fact he was so impressed with one of the sections that I scored, that he asked for all the sound effects to be removed on the soundtrack, so my music was more prominent".

The soundtrack was issued on General Music records originally and has subsequently been re-issued onto CD by Alhambra in Germany. General music or GDM as it is known today was founded by several prominent composers, Piccioni was one of these.

"I was the founder of the company, it was a record company, but more importantly it was a music publishing company. The other composers involved with the establishing of the company were, Ennio Morricone, Luis Bacalov and Armando Trovajoli. Enrico De Melias who became Morricone's manager was a partner. The company is still active today and has begun to re-issue several of its older soundtracks, some on its own label and others under license to various companies around the world".

Regarding CD re-issues, did the composer think that enough of his music was available on compact disc or record?

"No, never enough". (laughs).

Was he engaged on anything for the cinema or television now?

"Recently I have been working on a film with my good friend Alberto Sordi, this is a documentary which deals with the philoso-

phy and sociology of soccer, this will be aired by the Italian television network RAI, and then hopefully shown around the world".

Il Momenta Della Verita contained a wonderful score, which was a fusion of jazz flavours and symphonic styles. An original and unique way of scoring a movie. I asked the composer if he was asked to score the movie in this way, or did he decide to tackle the assignment like this?

"The ideas on this were all mine, I was in charge on this film for the music, the director left me to write what I wanted to".

When did the composer like to become involved on a film?

"As early as possible, but relay it is not good until the film is in its rough cut stage, if I am given a script, it is almost useless to me, as scripts change all of the time and are very rarely intact by the time that it comes to filming".

And in what order did he score a film, from start to finish, larger cues first or how did he tackle the work?

"I actually prefer to start from the end of the movie, I can then see the films climax and develop the rest of the score from there, maybe this seems a little odd to you, as many other composers work from the start of the film, but I find that this is the best way to work".

Did he conduct all his scores or just some of them?

"I conduct at least eighty percent of my music for film, but there have been times when circumstances that have arisen make it impossible for me to conduct, so I have someone else work with the orchestra, whilst I am in the recording booth, but I still supervise what is going on musically, and if I am not happy with something I am able to change it. By this I might think the music will work when I am writing it, but in the recording studio I might think "NO" this is not working".

My final question to the composer was what was the largest orchestra that he had ever employed?

"The largest orchestra that I have worked with so far is ninety seven players that included a sixty strong string section; this was for a ballet Stress, which was performed at the Lyric theatre in Palermo Sicily".

Piero Piccioni died on July 23rd, 2004, in Rome. He scored well over three hundred movies in his illustrious career.

GUIDO AND MAURIZIO DE ANGELIS.

Composing duo, Guido, and Maurizio De Angelis, wrote numerous scores for various genres of movies that were produced in Italy and Europe during the seventies through to the eighties. Their distinct and innovative sound has graced many a western, comedy and thriller over the years, their score for **They Still Call me Trinity** is held in high esteem by many collectors, and it was a joy to have the score finally released onto compact disc recently. I would like to thank both Guido and Maurizio for answering my many questions and a special thank you to Michela who was so helpful in liaising. The interview took place in 2018, when the composer/performers were planning more concerts and tours.

I think I am correct saying you began as performers and producers for RCA, how did you become involved with the scoring of films?

"It's true. We were members of the orchestra in RCA as session men, Maurizio playing guitar and Guido on flute. At that time, RCA made our orchestra play in all the most successful albums they produced. After a long period, they gave us the opportunity to be not only performers, but also arrangers of their productions. The first proposal came from Vincenzo Micocci, one of the greatest music producers of that time. The album we were asked to work on was Tanto pe' canta,' sung by Nino Manfredi, a famous Italian actor. This album had a huge success and Nino asked us if we'd like to write the music for his first film as director: Per grazia Ricevuta. We said yes, obviously. That's how our career as composers started. That's also how our career took off because that film and its soundtrack had a great success. Some of those songs were also used as opening themes in very popular radio shows such as Alto Gradimento by Renzo Arbore and Gianni Boncompagni company".

They Still Call Me Trinity, is considered a landmark score for you, and one of my own personal favourites, how much time did you have to score the movie, and where was the music recorded?

"Thank you We had about three months to do the entire work. The music was recorded at the RCA, B studio".

You are well known for your originality where music is concerned and for your effective use of songs in movies, when you are working on a project do you begin with a vocal theme and build the score around this or maybe you begin with the instrumental themes and then work on the song?

"At that time in the nineteen seventies the best course of action was to start from the main theme. In most cases, also at the request of the director, this was a vocal theme. The next step was to work on the instrumental versions of the main theme. The real score was composed at a later stage, once the film was edited, for optimization reasons".

Keoma- The Violent Breed was a big score for you, the vocal performances are unique, when you write a theme or a song do you have a particular artist in mind when you are writing or before you begin work on it?

"Not exactly and not always. Sometimes we realize we need a pop, rock, or country performer, only if agreed with the director. Then we look for the right artist with the help of the record label that has interests in the score".

What is your opinion at the state of film music today, compared with film music from earlier decades?

"It's a magic world where all expression possibilities can have a place. We need to find a way to strike a balance between the needs of the director, the producer, and the record label. Up until recently, film music revolved around the idea of "main theme": it was necessary to have a recognizable theme to identify and boost the plot of the movie. On the contrary, nowadays directors prefer "neutral" music, often based on sound design. The suggestive power of this music lies in sound and timbre, not in recognizable melodies. Music is effective and strengthens the feeling of each movie scene, but – without a real theme, a melody – can't exist out of the scene, autonomously. I don't know what the future holds, but new technologies will surely lead to new sounds and atmospheres. Even without a real theme, these can be very convincing; it depends on the kind of film and on the story, you want to tell".

Dogtanian, was an animated series you worked on, how did you become involved on this?

"The producer of that series, Claudio Biern of BRB Madrid, had heard lots of our music and liked it so hired us, he wanted a soundtrack that had a pop sound with a vocal that people could sing".

You have worked on TV series as well as movies, is there in your opinion a great difference between scoring a feature film and scoring a series of many episodes for TV?

"No, there's no difference at least not for us. Both for TV series and movies, music must express common elements: passion, adventure,

epic, suspense, intimacy, feelings, danger, action... Same ingredients, same proceedings".

What composers or artists would you say influenced or inspired you in the way you scored a film or wrote music?

"What we admire the most in composers is compositional brilliance and orchestration technique. Among non-Italians, we can mention John Williams, Thomas Newman, Hans Zimmer, James Newton, Howard, James Horner... For Italy, Ennio Morricone and Nino Rota".

Many your soundtracks have been issued onto CD and recently scores such as **They Call me Trinity, Valdez Horses,** and **Affyon Oppio,** have been released, do you have any involvement in what music will be going onto any of the releases, and is there a score of yours that has not been released that you would like to see available on a recording?

"No, we have no influence on the choices editors and producers made for these soundtracks. We composed music for different publishers and different record labels, and they act however they like. Most of our soundtracks issued on LP, except for a few that were not long enough like, for example, L'allenatore nel Pallone. In some cases, the label released only the main theme of a soundtrack, on 45, but composers have no part in these choices".

When you scored, **They Still Call me Trinity** were you given any specific instructions by the director as to what style or sound that he wanted?

"The director wanted a vocal theme for the opening credits, so we figured a song with a country atmosphere. We were very happy we could use the acoustic style we liked so much".

Do you think it is important for a film or a TV series to have a catchy theme or song?

"It depends on the director and/or the producer. Personally, we think that a recognizable theme, at least during the opening credits, should and could be in a film. It gives the series or the movie an identity that remains even outside the screening room. The tendency is now to reduce catchy themes, believing that they would distract the audience from what's happening in the scene. But this debate has no simple conclusion: there will always be advocates of both views".

How many times did you normally have to see a movie before you began to get any fixed ideas about where music should be placed or what style of music was needed?

"Sometimes we need to see it several times. We must understand the right mood we need to recreate in each situation. Then we must watch it again with the director, to have his opinion on where to place the music. Obviously, at this point we can fairly say what we would do and convince the director that it would be better to place music in one scene rather than in another. We also discuss the style of the music for each single scene".

I know you are both accomplished performers, so did you perform a lot of the work yourselves on your film scores?

"Yes. For instance, Maurizio usually plays the guitar main parts. Along with the orchestra, or in separate tracks before adding the rest of the instruments".

Using the TV series **Sandokan** as an example, when working on a series for television, do you score episodes in the order that they will be aired, or do you score more than one episode at a time, and do you on a long running series re-use any themes from early episodes in later ones?

"We work on one episode at a time. In some cases, to perfect the clarity and consistency of the music, we do reuse one or more tracks, edited accordingly".

What method do you use to work out your musical ideas, keyboard, guitar or piano?

"It depends on the genre. For orchestral and symphonic scores, for example, the initial idea becomes known at the piano. For more country or pop styles, the guitar is a perfect starting point".

What would you define as the purpose of music in film?

"It must increase the feelings and the emotions the footing shows, to put flesh on their bones. Or add new feelings and emotions if for some reasons, there's too few".

You are doing a comeback tour, although I don't think you ever went away really, where will you be performing?

"Thank you. We made a concert in Budapest, recently, and it was a great success. In the wake of that event, we've been proposed to do other live shows. So, our production company is planning another tour on which, of course, we will have our say. We'll communicate news and dates shortly".

The lyrics to some of your songs were written by Susan Duncan who is British politician Ian Duncan Smith's sister, how did you begin your collaboration with her?

"She was a staff member of the Foreign Office at RCA at the time of our first film scores. When we had the need, we asked her and her partner Cesare De Natale to write some lyrics for our songs as Oliver Onions. Since then, we worked together for a very long time".

Will we be hearing any new film scores from you soon?

"Yes. Something's coming, but it is too soon to realize what style the director will want, if epic or minimalist. We'll see".

NORA ORLANDI.

Nora Orlandi is unique within the film music world of the Italian western, not only is she a composer and the creator of the 4+4 choral group but she is the first female composer to work on Italian westerns and in Italian cinema. She is also an accomplished pianist, soprano and occasionally entered acting. Her younger sister Paola Orlandi is a singer songwriter.

Q: Where and when were you born?

"I was born in Voghera (Lombardia), Italy on the 28th of June 1933".

What musical education do you have?

"I studied at the academy of music in Voghera which is a Conservatorio".

 Did you come from a musical family background?

"My mother, Fanny Miriam Campos, was a great lyric singer. My father and my brother were merely enthusiastic for music, while my sister is a singer too. She collaborated with me as soloist and vocalist in both my two groups: the 2+2 and the 4+4. As for my present family, my husband is my most precious collaborator: he helps me in everything... last September we celebrated fifty five years of marriage! I have two sons and at least five nephews, aged from seven up to twenty two".

You began primarily as a singer in a group with Alessandroni. When did you decide to form your own singing group?

"To tell the truth the group was mine... and I gave to Alessandroni the possibility to join! He was one of my first vocalists. Subsequently I had the pleasure to work with Massimo Cini, one of my vocalists for thirty years, and there is Enzo Gioieni, who I have worked and performed with since the start of my career".

You have collaborated with many composers on film scores, who would you say was the most enjoyable to work with?

"Every composer or performer I have collaborated with I have enjoyed collaborating with, my collaborations have always been undertaken with enthusiasm and positivity, independently from the composer or the film. Passion is something you have inside, and I merely offered it to everyone that called me to work".

What was your first film score, and how did you progress from a performer to a composer?

"In 1953–54, at the age of twenty, I composed my first film score: Non Vogliamo Morire. I really don't remember the day I became a singer professionally: it is too far away".

Do you conduct all your own music, or do you sometimes have a conductor?

"No, on the contrary: my scores have always been directed by someone else more famous than me... for example Paolo Ormi and

Robbie Poitevin. Besides, I was busy with many other projects, and did not have enough time available to conduct my own music".

Do you think enough of your music from film has been released onto LP or CD?

"I have never paid much attention to that matter. Soundtracks are only thirty percent of my work, the rest was compounded by various performances, TV and radio-phonic shows, advertising spots... Moreover, I took part in about fifteen San Remo music Festivals".

How do you work out your musical ideas, do you use a piano or do you work with a synthesiser?

"I use neither a piano nor a synthesiser. I compose without any instrument and only at the end I check what I wrote with a piano. Only Mozart could write without checking".

How many times do you normally watch a movie before you start to get any fixed ideas about where the music will be placed and what style of music you will employ?

"Most of the times you must ask expressly to watch the film. Often it is sufficient to watch some parts of it, only one time, to under-stand the more suitable musical style. The music must be a "sound photography," parallel to the images; it depends really on each individual project".

How long did you normally get to work on a film score; you could use *The Sweet Body of Deborah* as an example?

"It depends on the kind of the job... I don't exactly remember how much time I got to work on a singular film score. It is too difficult to quantify it because I could not devote so much time to a sole work. As I have already said, soundtracks are not my priority, even though they are a way of artistic expression that I have a particular passion for myself".

Do you prefer to work on a particular type or genre of movie, or are you happy working on all types of subject matter?

"I am happy working on any type of film, because it is always a very interesting artistic experience. As spectator I love thrillers... but unfortunately, I haven't had the opportunity to do many of these".

Have you ever had a score rejected or have had to do a rush job on a film after another score had been discarded. And what is your opinion of contemporary film music?

"Thankfully, this has never happened, I am very fortunate. The film music of today is good... however, if it is music from yesterday or of today it is always film music: a "light" entertainment! This kind of music isn't a committed artwork, but a "light" artwork with a specific beauty".

Would you say that you were influenced by any composers, classical or film music composers?

"No, not really. For me to write music that is influenced by another composer would be very much like plagiarism, of course it is possible for this to be done unconsciously".

When a soundtrack recording is released on record or compact disc do you have any input into what music will go onto that release?

"When one of my soundtracks is released on record or CD, certainly I am very glad, but I'm not interested to intervene in the track's selection. Once I finished my work of music composition I spend my time with other projects. I'm very busy".

Do you orchestrate all your scores yourself?

"No, I don't. It depends by the situation, the needs… and, most of all, by the time I can spend in it, so sometimes I work on them myself other times not".

Are you working on anything now?

"Personally, I'm busying myself with some very interesting teaching projects… But I always take into consideration what people offer to me".

Nora Orlandi passed away in December 2024.

QUIÉN SABE?
GIAN MARIA VOLONTE'
KLAUS KINSKI
MARTINE BESWICK
LOU CASTEL
FERNANDEZ
DAMIANO DAMIANI
TECHNICOLOR - TECHNISCOPE

TONY ANTHONY
un UOMO
un CAVALLO
una PISTOLA
DAN VADIS
VANCE LEWIS
EASTMANCOLOR

ALBERTO GRIMALDI
FRANCO NERO
TONY MUSANTE IN
IL MERCENARIO
IL MERCENARIO
JACK PALANCE   GIOVANNA RALLI
TECHNICOLOR   TECHNISCOPE

EASTMANCOLOR   DORYSCOPE
GIULIANO GEMMA
ADIOS GRINGO
EVELYN STEWART
ROBERT CAMARDIEL - JESUS PUENTE
GRANT   JEAN   MAX   MONIQUE
LARAMY   MARTIN   DEAN   SAINT CLARE
PETER CROSS
GEORGE FINLEY

PRESENTA UN FILM PRODOTTO DA ALBERTO GRIMALDI
YUL BRYNNER
INDIO BLACK, SAI CHE TI DICO:
SEI UN GRAN FIGLIO DI...
DEAN REED · PEDRO SANCHEZ · SAL BORGESE · GERARD HERTER · FRANCO FANTASIA · JOSEPH PERSAUD · SUSAN SCOTT
CON GIANNI RIZZO
UN FILM DI FRANK KRAMER
TECHNICOLOR
TECHNISCOPE

GIULIANO GEMMA
e'
ARIZONA COLT
MICHELE LUPO

ENRICO MARIA
SALERNO
in
BANDIDOS

EL HALCÓN
Y LA PRESA
LEE VAN CLEEF - TOMAS MILIAN
WALTER BARNES - MARIA GRANADA - FERNANDO SANCHO
Dirigida por SERGIO SOLLIMA - Música de ENNIO MORRICONE
TECHNICOLOR - TECHNISCOPE

VIETATO AI MINORI DI 14 ANNI
BLINDMAN
TONY ANTHONY · RINGO STARR . BLINDMAN
LLOYD BATTISTA · MAGDA KONOPKA · RAF BALDASSARRE · AGNETA ECKEMYR
EASTMANCOLOR · SPES
FERDINANDO BALDI

original motion picture soundtrack in full stereo
un UOMO un CAVALLO una PISTOLA
THE STRANGER RETURNS
music composed and conducted by
STELVIO CIPRIANI

JOHN GARKO
SEAN TODD
I VIGLIACCHI
NON PREGANO
JOSE JASPE · MARIA MIZAR · MANUEL GALIANA
ELISA MONTES · TERRY WILSON · IVAN SCRATUGLIA · MIGUEL DEL CASTILLO · ALAN COLLINS
MARLON SIRKO
METHEUS FILM · COPERCINES
EASTMANCOLOR

DANCING

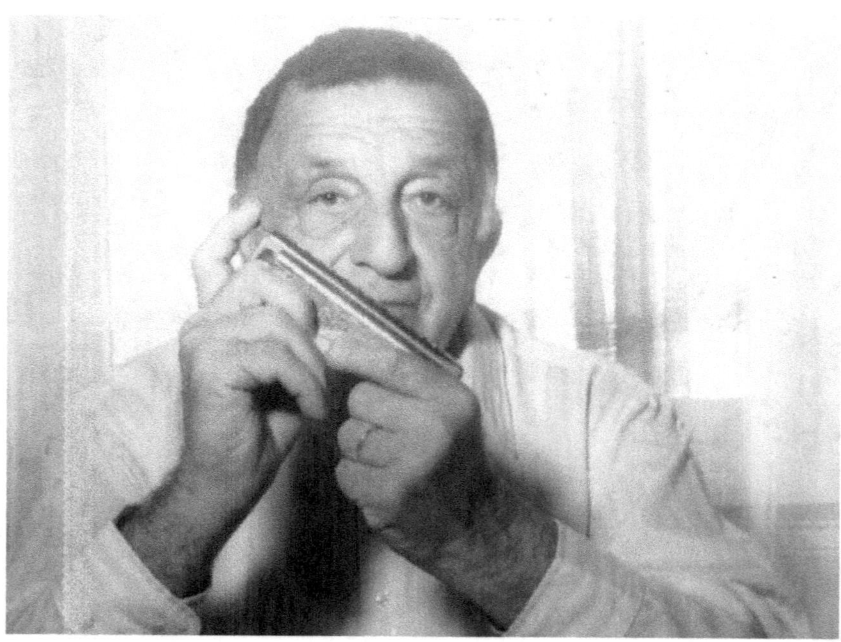

L' ITALIAN INTERNATIONAL FILM PRESENTA
ANDA MUCHACHO, SPARA!
FABIO TESTI · CHARO LOPEZ · JOSÉ CALVO · BEN CARRA · ROMAN BARETT · MASSIMO SERATO · EDUARDO FAJARDO
BRUNO DI GERONIMO · EDUARDO M. BROCHERO · ALDO FLORIO
BRUNO NICOLAI
ALFREDO NICOLAI · ROBERTO CINEMATOGRAFICA-ROMA
ALDO FLORIO · SCHERMO GIGANTE · TELECOLOR

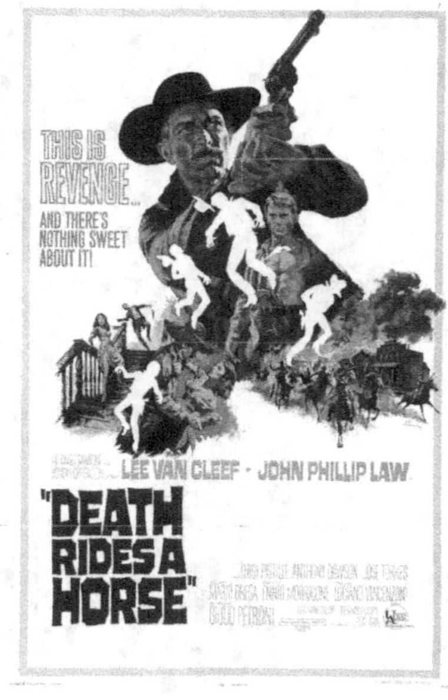
THIS IS REVENGE...
AND THERE'S NOTHING SWEET ABOUT IT!
LEE VAN CLEEF · JOHN PHILLIP LAW
"DEATH RIDES A HORSE"

TONY KENDALL
L'ODIO E IL MIO DIO

DEMOFILO FIDANI
TARQUINIA FILM s.r.l.
HUNT POWERS
QUEL MALEDETTO GIORNO D'INVERNO...
DJANGO E SARTANA
...ALL'ULTIMO SANGUE!
STET CARSON
DEAN STRATFORD · DENNYS COLT · JOEL MOORE · MICHAEL BRANK · LUCKY MC MURRAY · ROBERT DANNISH
SIMONE BLONDELL · CELSO FARIA   MILES DEEM   EASTMANCOLOR
SCHERMO PANORAMICO

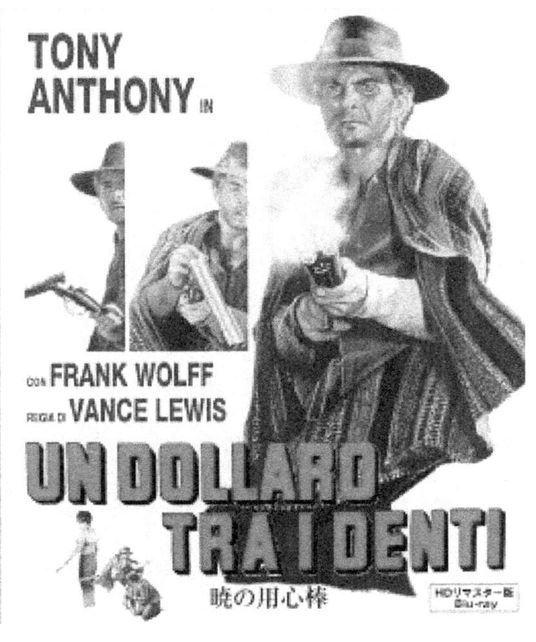
TONY
ANTHONY IN
CON FRANK WOLFF
REGIA DI VANCE LEWIS
UN DOLLARO
TRA I DENTI
暁の用心棒
HDリマスター版
Blu-ray

EURO INTERNATIONAL FILMS presenta
ROD STEIGER
JAMES COBURN
ROMOLO VALLI in
GIU' LA TESTA
MARIA MONTI
RICK BATTAGLIA
FRANCO GRAZIOSI
DOMINGO ANTOINE
ENNIO MORRICONE
SERGIO LEONE
TECHNICOLOR · TECHNISCOPE
GIU'
LA TESTA

ANTHONY STEFFEN · JOHN GARKO · ERIKA BLANC · CHARLES of ANGEL
1000 DOLLARI sul NERO
TECHNISCOPE
EASTMANCOLOR
SIEGHARDT RUPP · Angelica Ott · Daniela Igliozzi · Frank Farrell · Gianni Solaro
JERRY WILSON ... CARROL BROWN
un film di MARLON SIRKO diretto da ALBERT CARDIFF

THE 5-MAN ARMY

PEA
CLINT EASTWOOD
dans
un film de SERGIO LEONE
...ET POUR
QUELQUES
DOLLARS
DE PLUS
avec
LEE VAN CLEEF
GIAN MARIA VOLONTE
TECHNICOLOR
TECHNISCOPE

un film di
SERGIO LEONE
IL BUONO
IL BRUTTO
IL CATTIVO

ED I RINTOCCHI DELL' AVE MARIA
ACCOMPAGNAVANO IL CANTO DELLA SUA PISTOLA
IL PISTOLERO
DELL' AVE MARIA
LEONARD MANN · LUCIANA PALUZZI
PETER MARTELL · ALBERTO DE MENDOZA

Titanus
JOHN RICHARDSON
JOHN IL BASTARDO
CLAUDIO CAMASO · MARTINE BESWICK · LUISA DELLA NOCE · CLAUDIO GORA · FURIO MENICONI · GIA SANDRI
NADIA SCARPITTA · PATRIZIA VALTURRI · GLAUCO ONORATO · GORDON MITCHELL DANITA · NICO FIDENCO
ARMANDO CRISPINO   FRANCESCO VINCENZO GENESI · C.C. HERCULES

LOU CASTELL
¡MÁTALO!
LUIS DAVILA • CLAUDIA GRAVY • CORRADO PANNI • ANTONIO SALINES y DIANA SOREL CON LA COLABORACION DE ANA Mª NOE
DIRECTOR CESARE CANEVARI EASTMANCOLOR PANORAMICA
COPRODUCCION HISPANO ITALIANA
COPERCINES (MADRID) ROFIMA CINEMATOGRAFICA (MILANO)

SILENT...SUDDEN...VIOLENT!
FOR MONEY..
FOR PLEASURE..
FOR REVENGE..
HE DOESN'T CARE
WHY HE KILLS
OR HOW!
BURT REYNOLDS
"NAVAJO JOE"

RCA
440.751
(QL3 3)
Bande originale du film PARAMOUNT
VICTOR
STEREO
BANDE
ORIGINALE
DU FILM
IL ETAIT UNE FOIS DANS L'OUEST
ENNIO MORRICONE

GEORGE HILTON
UNO DI PIU'
ALL' INFERNO
PAUL STEVENS · CLAUDIE LANGE · GERARD HERTER
PAUL MULLER · CARLO GADDI   GIOVANNI FAGO   DEVON FILM - FLORA FILM
EASTMANCOLOR · CROMOSCOPE

HE'S JUDGE...JURY... EXECUTIONER!
THE MAN WITH THE GUNSIGHT EYES IS BACK!
LEE VAN CLEEF
"RETURN of SABATA"

EURO INTERNATIONAL FILMS PRESENTA
ELI WALLACH E TERENCE HILL IN
I QUATTRO
DELL' AVE MARIA
TECHNICOLOR   TECHNISCOPE
BUD SPENCER · BROCK PETERS   KEVIN MAC CARTHY
GIUSEPPE COLIZZI   CRONO

MONTGOMERY WOOD
UNA PISTOLA
PER RINGO
FERNANDO SANCHO · HALLY HAMMOND
NIEVES NAVARRO · ANTONIO CASAS
GEORGE MARTIN
DUCCIO TESSARI   LUCIANO ERCOLI · ALBERTO PUGLIESE
TECHNICOLOR
TECHNISCOPE
CINERIZ

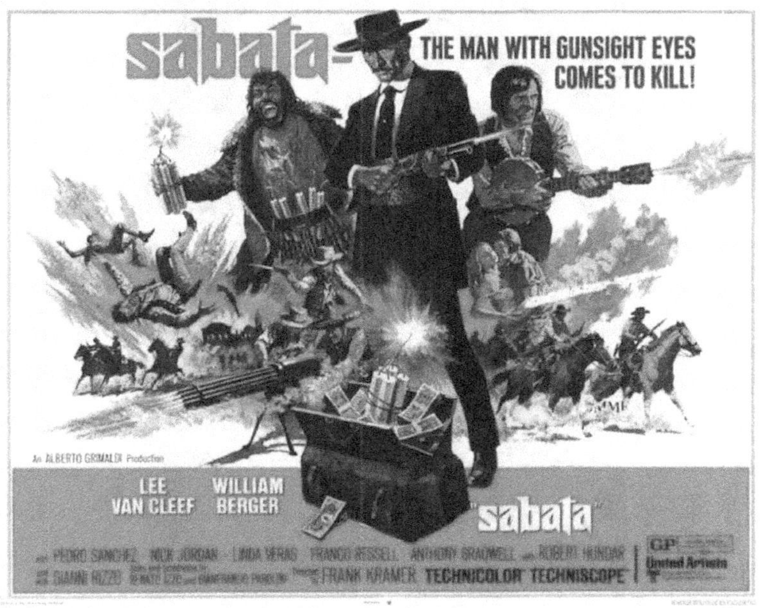
sabata-
THE MAN WITH GUNSIGHT EYES
COMES TO KILL!
An ALBERTO GRIMALDI Production
LEE
VAN CLEEF
WILLIAM
BERGER
"sabata"
PEDRO SANCHEZ   NICK JORDAN   LINDA VERAS   FRANCO RESSEL   ANTHONY GRADWELL   ROBERT HUNDAR
GIANNI RIZZO   RENATO IZZO   FRANK KRAMER   TECHNICOLOR   TECHNISCOPE
GP
United Artists

La I.F.C. INTERNATIONAL FILM COMPANY presenta una produzione B.L. VISION
ROBIN CLARKE
RICHARD CONTE
ENRICO MARIA SALERNO
ADOLFO CELI
TOMAS MILIAN
SENTENZA DI MORTE
ELEONORA BROWN
LILLI LEMBO • MONICA PARDO • LUCIANO ROSSI • BLANCO SCARLINI
Musica di GIANNI FERRIO
MARIO LANFRANCHI
TECHNICOLOR · TECHNISCOPE

EURO INTERNATIONAL FILMS
GIULIANO GEMMA.
...E PER TETTO UN CIELO DI STELLE
con MARIO ADORF
MAGDA KONOPKA · JULIE MENARD
GIULIO PETRONI · GIANNI HECHT LUCARI · DOCUMENTO FILM
EASTMANCOLOR · TECHNISCOPE

G.B. SA00 0005 STEREO
COLONNA SONORA ORIGINALE
SPARA GRINGO, SPARA
RAINBOW
musica di
S. M. ROMITELLI

RINGO
IL TEXANO
AUDIE MURPHY
BRODERICK CRAWFORD
DIANA LORYS

P.A.C. - LINEAFILM, CENTER VIDEO presentano
Regia di TONINO CERVI
Soggetto e Sceneggiatura
TONINO CERVI e DARIO ARGENTO
OGGI A ME...
DOMANI A TE!
BRETT HALSEY   WILLIAM BERGER   WAYDE PRESTON
BUD SPENCER e O'Banion

TERENCE HILL in
LO CHIAMAVANO
TRINITA'...
con ...BUD SPENCER
STEFFEN ZACHARIAS · DAN STURKIE · GISELA HAHN · ELENA PEDEMONTE
e con FARLEY GRANGER
DIRETTO DA E. B. CLUCHER   PRODOTTO DA ITA'O ZINGARELLI PER LA WEST FILM   COLORE DELLA TECNOSTAMPA

CHAPTER FOUR.

WESTERN INTO POP-ERA-THE SINGERS AND THE SONGS.

Before moving onto other composers involved with the Italian western genre, let us look at the use of songs within the genre. Often the title song from an Italian western would be released onto a 45rpm single record with a picture cover either showing a scene or poster from the movie in question or a picture of the vocalist of the song dressed as a cowboy. I suppose this in the early days was also a way of promoting the movie and its soundtrack, some of the songs from the films entering the hit parade or charts. The singles were mostly released in Italy, France, and Germany as in the beginning there was limited interest in the songs outside of these countries. Artists such as Maurizio Graf, Peter Tevis, Christy, Peter Boom, Raoul and others often appearing on RAI-TV.

Many soundtrack collectors in the UK never latched onto the Italian western theme song until RCA records released the compilation *Il Western* by Ennio Morricone onto an LP record, this included songs from *Gunfight at Red Sands, Seven Guns for the McGregor's, Bullets Don't Argue, A Pistol for Ringo* and its sequel *The Return of Ringo*. The songs from both Ringo movies becoming firm favourites with Italian western fans and Morricone devotees straight away. It was after the release of this compilation that collectors outside of

Italy began to take more notice of the title songs for the Italian westerns, and although composers such as De Masi, Fidenco, and Ferrio, had written songs before for their scores, these vocal versions of the themes gained more of a following. De Masi believed that it was essential for a western to have a title song. And his opening song *"Find a Man"* from **Quella Sporca Storia Nel West,** was to become one of the most popular and enduring from the genre.

The song, performed by Maurizio Graf, was co-written by Alessandro Alessandroni who also provided the infectious guitar riff that opened the performance. It also featured Il Cantori Moderni and an upbeat pop backing that resembled a Surf type song which was popular at the time in the USA, and also had a similar sound to tracks such as those recorded by the UK band The Tornadoes, so it was more like a track one would hear in a coffee bar in London rather than being from an Italian western. But this is how the song for the Spaghetti western evolved, composers combining the dramatic and conventional symphonic sounds of film scoring with the more contemporary sound of the sixties.

Another example of pop meets the Italian western is the opening vocal for Sergio Corbucci's **Django**, music by Luis Enriquez Bacalov. Which opened like De Masi's Find a Man vocal with a distinctive guitar riff, that led into an upbeat vocal performance supported by choir, percussion, and punctuating strings. Many of the songs were recorded in English which at times could be problematic because the vocalist being Italian did not have the correct pronunciation for some of the English words, at times this resulted in laughable performances. I for one, was always pleased to see the Italian recording included on the soundtrack. ***Django***, for example had both English and Italian versions, but the Italian language performance is instantly engaging and far more powerful and expressive. The vocal for this credited to Roberto Fia with the English version credited to Rocky Roberts. Roberts was an American vocalist and went onto work with composer Bacalov on a handful of other songs which included Can Be Done from the western ***Si Pio Fare...Amigo***. The English version of the song from ***Django*** was given a new lease of life more recently in Quentin Tarantino's ***Django Unchained,*** a film that was tracked with music from Italian scores.

Bruno Nicolai's rousing revolutionary themed opening song for ***Corri Uomo Corri*** is also worthy of a mention, performed on the original CAM vinyl release by Peter Boom, *"Espanto en el Corazon"* is sung in Spanish, the title translating to *Horror in the Heart*. It is a robust and lively affair, with Boom giving his all, sadly the song was not used on the opening titles of the movie, instead a different arrangement with actor Tomas Milian speaking and shouting the lyrics rather than singing them was used. This version was added to the soundtrack release in later years when the score was made available on digital platforms and an expanded compact disc was released. The Peter Boom performance is a more traditional sound rather than the pop driven flourishes of other examples, with Nicolai employing racing percussion, choir, clapping, and strings to evoke sounds that were associated with the Mexican revolution. Boom also performed the song on ***1000 Dollari Sul Nero-1000 Dollars on the Black***, for Michela Lacerenza, which was entitled *Necklace of Pearls.*

It is also worth mentioning that Morricone's theme for *A Fistful of Dollars* began life as a song. *Pastures of Plenty* (RCA PM45-3115) written by Woodie Guthrie and arranged by Morricone for singer Peter Tevis, was re-worked as an instrumental that eventually became the theme for the movie. The vocal parts being performed by whistler Alessandroni. Peter Tevis himself became a well-known figure in the world of the Italian western score, performing for the likes of Morricone, and De Masi, most notably on tracks such as *A Man Must Fight* from **Sette Dollari Sul Rosso-(Seven Dollars on the Red),** which evoked the sound of the Hollywood western score, with nods to Dimitri Tiomkin in-particular.

One of the most well-known songs from a Spaghetti Western is for the comedy **They Call Me Trinity,** the film was scored by Franco Micalizzi and Roberto Pregadio, instead of over top violence the movie contained a lot of visual comedy that often became slapstick. The up-beat and infectious title song was performed by Annibale Giannarelli, under the name of Annibale, with lyrics penned by British lyricist Lally Stott. It is a send up (as is the film) of the Italian western and the American western, drawing from both to create a parody of the genres.

The iconic vocal was an international hit and is still performed by Franco Micalizzi's big bubbling band in an instrumental arrangement when they are touring. The song was used more recently as the end title for Quentin Tarantino's **Django Unchained.**

Singer Raul or Raoul Lo Vecchio performed songs on numerous westerns, **Death Rides a Horse, A Taste of Death, 15 Scaffolds for a**

Murderer, 7 Winchester per Un Massacro, Quanto Costa Morire, I 4 Inesorabili, Ammazzali Tutti E Trorna Solo, Testa a Croce, Vado L'Amazzo E Torno, and many others. His distinct voice giving the songs an earthy and dramatic feel.

A firm favourite with collectors is his performance on *The Man from Nowhere,* by Francesco De Masi, and Alessandro Alessandroni for the movie **Arizona Colt** (1966). Don Powell too was a popular vocalist who regularly appeared on Italian western soundtracks, working with the likes of Marcello Giombini on **Tre Pistole Contro Cesare- (Death Walks in Laredo)** the title song "*Laredo*" was a fast paced piece, with Powell exaggerating and extending the word Laredo, to Lareeedo.

He also collaborated with composer Carlo Savina on **Pocchi Dollari Per Django (A Few Dollars for Django**) 1966, **Ehi Amigo..sei Morto** in 1971 and **Nevada** with Gianni Ferrio also in 1971. The singer collaborated with Angelo Francesco Lavagnino for the title song "*A Gambling Man*" on **5000 Dollari sul Asso-(5000 Dollars on the Ace)** 1964, and with Spanish composer Anton Garcia Abril on the classic **Texas Addio** in 1966. Powell's voice was at times compared with that of Frank Sinatra, having to it a smooth and mellow tone, a style that can be heard in his vocal for **Nevada** entitled "*They call it Gold*". Gianni Ferrio was a composer who was different from many other Italian Maestros who scored westerns, his music containing a jazz influence and having an inventive and innovative style, which could be seen as an alternative to the more familiar stock sounds of the spaghetti western soundtrack. Ferrio often combined elements of what was then established as Italian western music with that of a more classically slanted approach, the composer using solo trumpet, electric guitar etc but not in the same way as say Morricone, Nicolai, and Cipriani. This style of scoring can be heard in his excellent score for **Find a Place to Die**, the soundtrack contained two songs, both exceptionally good.

"Un Era Cowboy" and the title song for the film both of which were sung by Julia de Palma. Both had elements of classic Hollywood western scoring and Italian or European influences. *"Un Era CowBoy"* utilised choir, harmonica, strings and solo female voice that supported a seductive sounding vocal, with the title song **Find a Place to Die** being a more traditional ballad, that is essentially a love song. Guitar and strings combine to underline the powerful lyrics building to a crescendo that is filled with grandeur and romance.

Ferrio included many songs on his western scores, *"A Man A Story"* from **Un Dollar Bucato,** *"Golden Poker Kid"* from **Djurado**, *"That Man"* from **Mi Chiamavano Requiescat,** *"Let it Rain Let it Pour"* from **Amico Stammi Lontano Almeno Un Palmo,** and *"The Last Game"* from **Sentenza Di Morte** to list but a few.

INTERVIEW WITH SINGER AND ACTOR-PETER BOOM.

Vocalist Peter Boom appeared on the soundtracks to many Italian productions, his distinct voice gracing the credits of many an Italian western movie. But there is certainly more to this multi-talented man as I found out when I spoke to him during May and July in 2002.

Q; Had you always wanted to be a singer/songwriter?

"Oh, No, when I was in my early teens around thirteen or fourteen, I thought about studying theology, but by the time I reached my fifteenth birthday I had changed direction in my studies and moved onto psychology, I thought that this was more modern, and then at eighteen I left school to start my studies of Bel Canto".

So, what was your first encounter with singing on a film soundtrack?

"Well, I first did a test or audition for RAI, which is the Italian TV and Radio service, this went very well, in fact the members of the selecting committee that were auditioning me all stood and applauded my trial performance, which if I remember correctly was two songs, All the Way, and Old Man River. Unfortunately, I did not get any work out of this success, RAI worked on a recommendation system, and as I did not really know that many well placed people at the time like politicians or Cardinals, I found it very difficult to get anyone to sponsor me. It was some six months after my audition for RAI that I was asked to do another test, this time for CAM records which led to singing on Corri Uomo Corri. But an alternative version sung by the star of the movie Tomas Milian was used instead on the movie or at least on certain prints".

Was this originally destined for the score and when you recorded the song who was the conductor?

"No, Milian insisted on recording a version of the song, I felt bad about this, as I thought that he did not sing it well. At the sessions, the orchestra was conducted by Morricone. This was because Nicolai who had written the music was conducting the music for another movie which had music by Morricone these sessions had overrun so Morricone stepped in".

You also performed a song for the first *Sabata* movie, which had music by Marcello Giombini, but this was cut from the film, and has only just re-emerged on the new compact disc version of the score, why was this cut?

"I don't actually recall the song for Sabata, I think it was something in German, and maybe it was cut from certain prints of the movie, the producer of the new compact disc Lionel Woodman assures me that it is me, but I still am not one hundred percent sure, maybe I should ask Giombini himself".

Have you kept in contact with Giombini because you did collaborate with him on a few projects for the cinema?

"We lost contact a long time ago, but I am glad to say have recently got in touch again, we both keep promising to meet up but as yet this has not been possible, he now lives in Assisi in Italy, and concentrates on the writing of sacred music, he also writes books, which is something that I also do, so we are a strange pair of artists".

At the beginning of the *Sabata* main theme there is a mischievous laugh, was this you can you recall?

"You know, I honestly do not remember, by that time I had sung on so many soundtracks it was hard to keep a track on them".

Did you prefer collaborating with any composer or composers?

"Armando Trovajoli was very nice, I did three songs with him on a film called Il Giovane Normale, which turned out to be the only film made by Dino Risi that did not do well at the box office. I must say that I found it very enjoyable working with all the composers".

So, were you as a singer, under exclusive contract to CAM records?

"Yes, I was, but they would only ever pay me an advance for each song, which was about 50,000 lire. I never got a percentage of the sales or the total monies that the record made, and royalties were never passed onto me. In fact, CAM did not even inform me that Corri Uomo Corri had been re-issued onto CD. Guisseppe Giacchi who was one of the main people at CAM during the early years told me that my records sold particularly well in Japan".

I have always been curious about Giusseppe Giacchi, his name appeared on all of CAM's early releases I think as producer, did you have much contact with him whilst under contract to the company?

"Count Giusseppe Giacchi, was the driving force behind CAM. It was he who built up the company's immense repertoire of soundtracks, which is a real treasure trove of music. He parted company with the label in the seventies I think, I am not sure why, but the parting was a little sour. I met him again recently and he now produces programmes for television. I am thankful to him because it was, he who initially approached me to go and work for CAM".

Would you like to see the CAM western songs LP re-issued onto CD?

"Oh yes, of course I would. It would be good to have a re-edited and re-mastered version available on compact disc. But I don't think that this will happen".

Could you tell me what was your most successful record in sales?

"I was never informed as to how many copies of a single or LP had been sold. But my own personal view is that Corri Uomo Corri must be the most popular, but as for actual figures I do not know".

Have you ever given any concerts?

"Yes, I gave many concerts and enjoyed doing so. I also worked as a master of ceremonies on many occasions".

As an actor did you ever have a part in an Italian western?

"No, surprisingly enough I never worked in any westerns as an actor".

I do not know if I am correct or not, but I understand that you once worked as a private investigator.

"You must be a good investigator yourself if you unearthed that information. Yes, I did work as a PI, this was in Rome and Milan, I did this to finance my studies, and later especially in the early 1970s I had many, many professions to try and fill in all the financial gaps, which is something that I am still doing today".

You also dubbed the Italian voice of Ron Moody's Fagin character for the film musical Oliver; did you do this often on other films?

"Oh, yes that was a job that I enjoyed immensely, I liked to do this the most, I think. They had tried out so many Italian actors/singers for this part and I was the one that they selected. I did on other movies but cannot remember the titles; again, this was because I was very busy".

Many composers who wrote for the Italian western, have in recent interviews admitted that their music has not stood up to the test of time, a few of them saying that they are a little embarrassed by their efforts on certain movies, how do you feel about your contributions to the genre?

"Well certainly not embarrassed, this was a very positive and nice period of my life and career. I feel very positive about my contribu-

tions to this genre of films. My career did however take a downturn in the summer of 1972, this was when I produced and sang Come out and Love Him which was the first ever gay record in Italy, it was this that really cost me my career as a singer. For me this was a big tragedy, caused by marginalization, which effectively spoilt more than half of my life".

Did you ever use an alias on a film?

"I did at certain times use an alias, but there again so did many Italian film music composers, but on many occasions, I never received any type of credit for my performance, on Oliver for example and on a RAI TV film Noah, the technicians were credited but not any of the singers, disgraceful, I think".

CHAPTER FIVE.

SCREAMING THEMES.

From the title song or songs that were written and performed for Italian westerns, to the quirky, inventive, and pioneering themes that were penned by many of the composers who worked within the genre. It is only fitting that we should straight away mention the work of Ennio Morricone. Morricone's output in the world of film music was vast and affecting, so it is very surprising that a genre or style of music that his best remembered for (The Western) takes up a small portion of his output. ***The Grand Silence, The Big Gundown, A Pistol for Ringo, They Call Me Nobody, The Genius, Death Rides a Horse, The Five Man Army, Once Upon A Time in the West, Duck you Sucker, Bullets Don't Argue, Tepepa, and the Dollar movies.*** He also scored westerns such as ***Two Mules for Sister Sara, Guns for San Sebastien*** and more recently ***The Hateful Eight*** which were not Italian productions, but did have elements of the successful formula as applied by Italian filmmakers.

Morricone had a knack of creating a theme that stayed with the watching audience, and even when they left the cinema it was recalled easily and became like an ear worm. But the same can be said of the music for the entire genre of the Italian western, let's face it a western produced in Italy would not have made such an impact without its musical score. Music and images working together as they did in these Italian productions had not really been seen or heard before, and it is possible that we will never be affected and influenced by a genre's music in this way again. In new movies there is rarely a theme, or if there is it is short lived and unmemorable. In recent decades we must make do with the humming and dronelike sounds that are referred to as soundscape or sound design. But is sound design still something that can be categorized as scoring a movie? And is sound design something new?

Well yes in many ways I suppose that it is, instead of music sounds are placed on the film's soundtrack, or at least this is how it was explained to me. We could therefore argue that Italian western composers, directors, and producers were pioneers in using sound design. The use of sounds is evident in the ingenious opening sequence from **Once Upon a Time in the West,** not one note of actual music graces the opening credits, instead natural sounds are utilized, water dripping, a windmill turning, a fly buzzing, a telegram machine chattering away etc, it was a brilliant idea to use these for what is essentially the main title of the movie. The sounds combine with the images to raise the tension and introduce us to the waiting men at the station, heightening the audience's expectation about who they are waiting for. Sounds also played an important part within all the movies in the genre, wind blowing, people talking loudly, doors banging, burping, loud eating, odd sounding gunshots, and over the top sounds in fist fights, these along with the offbeat plots, the way in which directors shot movies, were all the trademarks of the spaghetti western, and in many ways are just as important as the musical scores.

But, to go back to the themes from Italian westerns, and to composers such as Luis Bacalov, Bruno Nicolai, Stelvio Cipriani, Carlo Rustichelli, Nico Fidenco, and so many more. The scores for the movies were very thematic, one must only listen to the music for ***Once Upon a Time in the West***, Morricone providing themes for all of its main characters, *Harmonica,* which is self-explanatory, *Cheyenne,* a plodding cowboy theme for banjo and whistler, that at times takes on a more threatening persona with hissing strings augmenting the banjo, *Jill,* underlined with the beautifully lyrical and soaring vocals of Edda dell Orso, and *Frank* the villain with fuzzy sounding guitar and those sinewy and sinister sounding strings. The Maestro employing these either separately when the character is on screen or about to enter from the wings, then combining elements of each when there is a confrontation or a scene with two or more central characters present.

The music for the movie ***Spara Gringo Spara***, is also a good example of this type of scoring the entire soundtrack is made up of themes that accompany either characters or locations. Composer Santa Maria Romitelli's pop driven soundtrack has upbeat percussion and rhythmic backgrounds that underline and support a rock orientated electric guitar and sweeping strings, is a prime example of the motif or theme deployment in Italian westerns. It was not just Romitelli that utilised this method to great effect, Nico Fidenco too, fused pop sounds with that of symphonic drama and suspense in his scores for movies such as ***John Il Bastardo, One more for Hell, To the Last Drop of Blood, Ringo the Texican***, and ***Bury them Deep***.

So we have established that themes played an important part within the soundtracks of Italian westerns, and these were not restricted to just the opening titles. In fact, when listening to an Italian western score one can pick out various tracks that could function as a central theme or a main theme for a movie rather than being part of a score.

Morricone's score for **The Good the Bad and The Ugly**, has compositions such as **The Ecstasy of Gold**, and **The Trio**, as well as its opening theme. Another theme that stands out is **Gunmen of the Ave Marie,** it is the epitome of the Italian western sound, whistle, guitar, choir, soaring trumpet solo, all combine to create a piece that is easily identified as being from the genre. Franco Micalizzi and Roberto Pregadio, collaborated to bring it to fruition and it has everything, that a spaghetti western theme requires. Then we have the more melodic theme as in **A Man Called Noon** and **The Grand Duel** both written by Luis Enriquez Bacalov, the former a romantic sounding piece dominated by strings, with the composer underlining these with chimes, subdued percussion, and woods, that are further embellished by horns, and in later arrangements the vocal excellence of Edda Dell Orso.

But these lighter moments were rare occurrences in scores for spaghetti westerns, with the emphasis being placed upon savage sounds, as in the screams at the beginning of **Navajo Joe**, the pulsating theme that mimics wild animals for **The Big Gundown,** and the earthy but alluring vocals of Gianna Spagnola on **The Hills Run Red.**

These examples were certainly not in any way paying homage to Aaron Copeland, as Hollywood composers had done in the past on western scores, but instead were establishing a unique sound and identity of their own. What I find very surprising with most Italian western scores is that they sound so grand in places, but they are performed by small orchestras or ensembles, sometimes of less than fifty players, the composers cleverly overdubbing certain instruments at key points within the scores.

Day of Anger for example sounds grand, loud, brash, and raw, but when you listen closely there are two maybe three guitars, a small brass section, strings, timpani and percussion, all recorded with a reverberating echo effect that makes it sound bigger than it is. The music for Italian westerns was as hardnosed and brutal as the films it was written for, and because of its originality it influenced and inspired generations of composers that followed.

CHAPTER SIX.

THE SETTLING OF ACCOUNTS-WHEN THE MUSIC STOPS YOU DIE.

The gunfight in an Italian western is often an impressive event, a time in the movies that was the ultimate settling of accounts, as in the central protagonists face off with each other in a final showdown, a dance of death, where in most cases only one or maybe two will be left standing at the end. The gunfight is the apex and final act of many films within the genre, and a time when the music took on a special and important role. It was in the scenes or sequences that music became foreground rather than background to the action, providing crucial support and punctuation to the scenes, and becoming a greater part of the filmmaking and creative process. The role that the soundtrack played in ninety nine percent of these sequences was vital. From Morricone's soaring trumpet solos, percussive echoes, and a death knell performed on guitar in *The Good the Bad and The Ugly's*, *"The Trio"*, to the same composer's tense and nervous cue *"La Resa"* in *The Big Gundown* which adds atmosphere and apprehension to the scene. Each piece very different, but in theory doing the same job in the specific scene, adding apprehension, anxiety, and heightening the excitement of each shootout.

The music at times also became part of the narrative as in *For A Few Dollars More* with the chiming watch, being a central part of the film's storyline, thus Morricone took the chiming watch and used it in his score, the music then becoming an extension of the narrative. This however is something that was not just a trademark of Morricone.

Composer Marcello Giombini, put this practise to effective use in **Sabata**, with one of the central characters Banjo seen on screen playing a banjo or an organ before he guns down his opponent. After watching the film Giombini incorporated these instruments into his score and orchestrated them into the fabric of his music for the movie. But it was Morricone who was the expert at this with the use of the Harmonica in **Once Upon a Time in the West** and the watch chimes in **For Few Dollars More.** Both being in normal circumstances everyday sounds, but in the hands of Morricone, the harmonica becomes menacing, and sinister, and the chimes are seen as time running out for one of the protagonistsin the showdown, and a reminder to one of the films central characters, Colonel Mortimer (Lee Van Cleef) of a murdered family member.

Many Italian westerns included a gunfight scene that was out of the ordinary or quirky, which was a breath of fresh air for cinema goers who had become accustomed to the stand-offs in American and German made westerns. In an Italian western it was very rarely a stand in the street shootout or if it was, other elements were involved that made it more interesting for the watching audience. The films also had novel ways of signalling when the draw should take place when the scenes were not scored. **Indio Black** or **The Bounty Hunters** is one example of this. When a weathervane is sent spinning by the central character Sabata played by Yul Brynner, the sign to draw and shoot is when the squeaking object stops.

Then there is a combination of actions and music in movies such as **Anda Muchaco Spara** or **Dead Men Ride,** in which a bag of gold is split open, the signal to shoot is when it has emptied, the action being accompanied by a soaring trumpet solo penned by Bruno Nicolai.

In Sergio Sollima's **The Big Gundown**, there are two face offs at the end of the movie, one between the bounty hunter Corbett (Lee Van Cleef) and a Prussian Baron (Gerard Herter) complete with monocle, which is accompanied using the music of Beethoven that composer Ennio Morricone cleverly adapts and weaves together with a Spanish guitar solo. The Beethoven Bagatelle no 25 in A minor being used as the theme for the Baron. The other showdown is between the character Cucillo (Tomas Milian) who the audience have seen as the villain throughout and the real villain of the piece Chet Miller (Angel Del Pozo). Morricone employs what sounds like a horn but is in fact a bass trumpet, which is underlined by choir, piano, castanets, strings, woods and percussion that build cautiously into a powerful composition that ends in an exciting almost shimmering crescendo whilst the protagonists face each other one with a gun the other with a knife.

Another example of the music becoming foreground instead of a background to the action is from the Sergio Corbucci Zapata western **A Professional Gun**. The end scene is superbly filmed and wonderfully scored by Morricone and Nicolai, with Alessandroni's distinct and flawless whistle, Il Cantori Moderni, bass electric guitar, solo trumpet, percussive elements and a stirring string arrangement. The "*Arena*" composition from this score is for me personally the peak of the duel or shootout scoring technique, it also brings together three of the principal themes of the score, for the three protagonists that are involved. There are also occasions when music is not used as in ***Today it's you Tomorrow me***, when the final duel with the Japanese bad guy takes place there is no music, but it is still an effective scene. The tension being created via clever camera shots and an eerie and tense silence on the soundtrack.

CHAPTER SEVEN.

COMPOSER PROFILES.

BRUNO NICOLAI.

Apart from Ennio Morricone, Bruno Nicolai is the composer/conductor that most soundtrack collectors and film buffs alike associate with the music for the Italian cinema, particularly the scores for the Spaghetti western genre. His style was not unlike that of Morricone's and at times it was very difficult to differentiate between the two composer's works for film and television. So much alike were their styles that many people outside of Italy during the late sixties and early seventies were of the opinion that Nicolai and Morricone were one and the same person, this opinion was also reinforced in the eyes of collectors because Bruno Nicolai conducted Morricone, s scores and his name appeared regularly alongside Morricone's on screen.

Bruno Nicolai was born in Rome in 1926. He studied with Aldo Manitia for piano and Antonio Fernandi and Godfredo Petrassi for composition. Petrassi was also responsible for schooling Morricone in composition, and that is why the two composers had similar styles in composition and orchestration. Nicolai also studied organ with Ferruccio Viganelli. Nicolai, s entry into film music as a composer came in 1963 when he scored **Head of the Family**, then in

1964 he collaborated on the score for the sequel to **Mondo Cane, Mondo Cane 2**. The composers break into bigger projects came in 1965 when Ennio Morricone asked him to conduct the score for Sergio Leone's **For a Few Dollars More,** after this Nicolai and Morricone worked on numerous projects together, Nicolai either being musical director or collaborating with Morricone on the composition of scores such as **Operation Kid Brother** and **A Professional Gun.** In 1966 he conducted Morricone's classic score for **The Good the Bad and the Ugly Good,** after this Nicolai began to work as a composer in his own right and started to be commissioned to write scores for all types of movies. As well as composing soundtracks for the cinema, Nicolai conducted many works for film, and during his career was employed by many well-known Italian film music composers, these included, Ennio Morricone, Nino Rota, Luis Bacalov and Carlo Rustichelli. Nicolai also had a keen interest in classical music and spent much of his time studying the scores of past musical experts such as Beethoven and Mozart. He also would at times perform on soundtracks for movies; this was in the main as a keyboard player or an organist. Nicolai would often be offered scores for movies when Morricone was not available.

So, at times he would be conducting for Morricone, playing organ for Rustichelli whilst at the same time composing a score of his own for a western or another genre. In 1969, Nicolai penned the soundtrack for an American produced western entitled **Landraiders**; this contained a particularly haunting theme and a driving and powerful main score. This is Nicolai, s best western score, and although it contains passages and musical phrases that are very much in the style of Morricone, most of the soundtrack is pure Nicolai. Morricone, s success unfortunately overshadowed much of Nicolai, s musical output, and many collectors and critics alike considered Bruno Nicolai to be a mere Morricone clone. This of course is not true, and Nicolai was a great composer possessing much originality and talent. One only must listen to his music for the movies as produced by filmmaker Jesus Franco. **Il Conte Dracula, 99 Women** and **Throne of Fire** being noteworthy examples. Nicolai, s scores for Italian made westerns are also of a very high quality, and contain many of the musical sounds and trademarks that are associated with the genre, but they also have a secondary sound that is similar to the music that was employed in American made westerns which is grandiose, sprawling, and vigorous, and this style combined with the rawness and savagery of the established spaghetti western score creates an interesting and original sound.

During the 1970's Nicolai established his own recording label, this was for the purpose of releasing his own film scores and other musical works, a small an independent label Edi-Pan released a number of albums, but was not really that widely distributed, and this is probably why Nicolai's soundtracks were always difficult to obtain outside of Italy in the days of vinyl. The label still operates today, and is helmed by the composer's daughter Julia, she took charge of things when her father passed away in August 1991, but now licences music rather than release it. Since his death many of the Maestro's soundtracks have made an appearance on compact disc. He died on August 16th, 1991, he was just sixty five. Unfortunately, the composer's death went almost unnoticed, and most soundtrack collectors that were aware of his music did not receive news of the composer's death until some two months later. His passing left a void in the Italian film music fraternity, a void that in many opinions has never been filled.

GIANNI FERRIO.

Gianni Ferrio was born in Vicenza, Veneto, Italy on the 15th of November 1924. He originally intended to become a doctor and began to study medicine during the 1950's completing his studies at the University of Padua. However, the composer soon realized that it was music that he was destined to be involved with and not medicine. He studied violin with Mariano Frigo and expanded his musical studies to harmony, composition, and musical direction under the tutelage of Amerigo Girotto and Arrigo Pedrollo.

In 1953 the composer began an intensive period of recording activity with the CGD in Milan. He collaborated with many artists during this period of his career these included Teddy Reno, Jula de Palma, and Johnny Dorelli. In 1959, Ferrio scored his first motion picture, which was a war/comedy, **Guardatele ma non Toccatele**, the movie starred Ugo Tognazzi and Johnny Dorelli and was directed by Mario Mattoli. This was followed by **Tipi da Spiaggia** in the same year, which was also directed by Mattoli and had Tognazzi in the leading role. In 1960, Ferrio scored his first western movie entitled **Un Dollaro di Fifa** the movie was another comedy and was directed by Giorgio Simonelli and yet another vehicle for actor Ugo Tognazzi, although produced in Italy this was not what is now referred to as a spaghetti western as it was released before the Italian western genre as we know it had been created. The 1960's was a busy and fruitful period for Ferrio, he wrote the music for numerous motion pictures during this period and began to create his own unique sound as a composer starting to put his own distinctive musical stamp upon numerous examples of films which encompassed many genres. Like so many Italian composers who worked in film during this period Ferrio scored many westerns at this time and although he was a composer that was involved heavily with this genre he never really conformed to the utilization of the "Italian western sound"

In fact, it is true to say that Ferrio created his own unique sound for the westerns he worked upon, on many occasions infusing a style that was jazz orientated. Unlike many of the other Italian composers that were active at this time, Ferrio very rarely collaborated with any other writer on his scores, in fact the one thing that linked Ferrio to others involved in the western genre was the choir Il Cantori Moderni, as Ferrio often used these and their director Alessandroni on his soundtracks. He did collaborate with Ennio Morricone on **Fort Yuma Gold**, but this was we are told not a collaboration in the true sense of the word, meaning that each composer contributed compositions to the movie, with Ferrio's contribution being the greater.

The composer scored many key examples within the Italian western genre, these included, **Sentence of Death, Desperado, Per Pochi Dollari Ancora, Joe Cerati Un Posto Per Moire, El Durado, Amico Stammi Lontano Almeno Un Palmo,** and one of the last Italian westerns produced **California**. Ferrio's style is instantly recognisable, the composer making excellent use of the percussive elements of the orchestra, he invariably combines percussion and wood-wind to achieve a dramatic and highly original sound. As well as writing for the cinema the composer has contributed numerous scores to television productions and worked prolifically as a song writer, composer, and musical director for artistes such as, Astor Piazzolla, Toots Thieleman, Luis Bonfà, James Taylor, Jerry Lewis, Mina, Caterina Valente, Ellis Regina, Ornella Vanoni, Milva and Gigi Proietti. His music has enhanced and supported approximately one hundred and twenty movies and as many television projects, collaborating with many directors, including: Ermanno Olmi, Luigi Zampa, Miklós Jancsó, Giorgio Capitani, Steno, Duccio Tessari, Sergio Corbucci, and Marco Ferreri. In his latter career Ferrio remained active and conducted the Roma Sinfonietta Orchestra in several concerts. Ferrio is in every sense chameleon like when it comes to scoring motion pictures as he is happy writing for, Westerns, Giallo, s, Comedies, Sex and psychedelic capers, Romantic tales and horror and adventure stories. He is an original and an accomplished composer but considering his immense output it is surprising that he is still almost unknown outside of Italy and the European continent, unless of course you happen to be talking to a fan of Italian film music. The Maestro passed away on October 21st, 2013. He will be missed greatly....

LUIS ENRIQUEZ BACALOV.

Luis Bacalov was born on August 30th, 1933, in Buenos Aires Argentina, moving to Italy later. He contributed much to the genre of the western and Italian cinema in general. His scores for westerns that were produced in Italy were consistently good and at times highly thematic, although the composer did tend to borrow from himself on many of his western scores. By this I mean he would reprise various cues from films such as *Django* and *A Bullet for the General* in later works for the genre. His theme for the movie *Django* directed by Sergio Corbucci, is one of the genres best known non-Morricone themes. Bacalov often worked with Alessandroni and the choir Il Cantori moderni, thus creating a sound that was not unlike the style that had been created by Morricone. In fact, Morricone functioned as musical supervisor on the composers score for *A Bullet for the General.* Bacalov also worked with Morricone on the score for *Per Amore*, performing pianoforte. The composer worked steadily in the Italian film music arena during the late 1960's and into the 1990's when he scored *Il Postino* for which he received an Oscar. His last scoring assignment was in 2014. The composer scored many successful movies such as *We Still Kill the Old Way, A Question of Honour, The Judge,* and the excellent *Cuori Solitari* to list but a few. He scored over two hundred movies and TV series and movies made for television in his career. Westerns which he worked on included: *A Man Called Noon, They Call him King, The Grand Duel, Gold for the Bravados, Sugar Colt, A Bullet for the General,* and *Django*. He died in Rome on November 15th, 2017.

MARCELLO GIOMBINI.

Marcello Giombini was born in Rome Italy on July 24th, 1928, from a very early age Giombini would practice playing organ in several of the churches in the Italian capital. Whilst he was gaining experience at becoming proficient in playing the organ he also began to study musicology and philology and would research both subjects within the vast libraries that were available in Rome. Giombini is predominantly known for his compositions for the world of film, but the composer also wrote numerous pieces for concert hall performance which he became in demand for during the 50's and 60's when a number of his compositions were performed by the RAI orchestras which were broadcast on both television and radio, some of these being broadcast live. He began to write for the cinema in the early part of the 1960's his first film score is recorded as *Vulcano-Filgio di Giove* in 1961 which was directed by Emimmo Salvi, he continued to write quite prolifically for the cinema through to the 1980's his last score for a movie being in 1984 for *Le Schiave di Caligola* directed by Lorenzo Onorati.

Giombini made some important contributions to the genre of the Italian western, *Sabata, Return of Sabata, Garringo, Acquasanta Joe, Ballata per un Pistolero* among them. Giombini also provided a fully electronic score for *Il Mio Nome E Scopone E Faaccio Sempre Cappotto* in1972 for filmmaker Juan Bosch, which was the last Italian produced western to star Anthony Steffen. The Maestro contributed strong soundtracks for many varying genres and was able to adapt to each scenario. Giombini functioned as director of The Chorus of the Roman Philharmonic Academy with whom he recorded a disc of renaissance music this included an edition of the story of music which was commissioned by RCA under the direction of Cesare Valabrega. The maestro was also responsible for researching the edition of the resurrection of the body of The Knights of Emilia. In Giombini's opinion the turning point in his career came with the composition of the mass of the young for shouting, guitars, keyboard, and percussion, which received its premiere performance in the oratory of San Black Filippo on April 25th, 1966. The composer dedicated himself to the composition of sacred music, in the last years of his life, and in 2002 recorded several Psalms taking his inspiration from the contemporary musical palette and combined a new age style of music with Biblical texts. The composer was also a pioneer in the field of electronic music and worked on a few science fiction movies adding his own innovative style of electronic pop to the proceedings; he wrote film music under the alias of Pluto Kennedy and at times went under the assumed name of Marcus Griffin. After the 1980's Giombini seemed to become something of a recluse and would not discuss his music for film at all. He composed the music for well over eighty motion pictures and it is sad that many of these shining examples of Italian film music remain unpublished. He died in Assisi on December 12th, 2003.

MICHELE LACERENZA.

Born in Taranto, Puglia, Italy on January 7th, 1922. Michele Lacerenza was to become one of the most important musicians to relate to the Italian cinema and in- particular the Italian western. Like Alessandroni, s whistle and guitar playing, Franco De Gemini's excellent harmonica performances and Edda Dell Orso's unique aural vocalising, Lacarenza was to make his mark on the western genre and other movie scores with his inspired and unblemished trumpet playing.

Lacerenza came from a family background that was musical; his Father Giacomo Lacerenza was a well-known conductor. Lacerenza came to the forefront of Italian film music when he was asked by composer Ennio Morricone to perform trumpet on **A Fistful of Dollars,** the film's director Sergio Leone had originally insisted on having Italy's most prominent trumpet player at that time Nini Rosso to perform on the soundtrack, but Morricone wanted to use Lacerenza because he remembered his flawless performances whilst they were at the music conservatory and has stated since that he wrote the piece with Lacerenza's trumpet in mind.

After playing the films central theme for Leone the great filmmaker was said to be reduced to tears because Lacerenza's performance was so full of emotion. Morricone described him as "*A sublime trumpet player*" After the success of **A Fistful of Dollars,** Lacerenza continued his collaboration with Morricone on scores such as **A Pistol for Ringo, For a Few Dollars More**, and **The Good the Bad and The Ugly**. Lacerenza became much in demand and began to perform on many other film soundtracks, it was also at this time that he had a hit record with a cover version of The House of the Rising Sun (La Casa Del Sole) a song that had been a worldwide hit for British rock band The Animals.

Lacerenza's career went from strength to strength and as well as performing on film scores and collaborating with composers such as Ennio Morricone, Nino Rota and Armando Trovajoli he also began to compose music for the cinema and although his output may not have been immense it was certainly important and original. His scores for *L'Ira di Dio* and *1000 Dollari Sul Nero* being stand out examples. The Maestro also taught music at the Foggia Conservatory of music and the Santa Cecilia Academy. He died in Rome on November 17th, 1989.

BENEDETTO GHIGLIA.

Italian composer Benedetto Ghiglia was born on December 27th, 1930, in Fiesole Italy. Information about this Italian Maestro has been very difficult to obtain as he has for most of his career avoided interviews and press releases. He came from a family that was very musically orientated, his Father was Oscar Ghiglia renowned and respected classical guitarist. Ghiglia began to score motion pictures during the early 1950's, his first soundtrack being for a documentary *Delta Pardano*. He then scored on another short documentary film *Madrigale d'Attunno* in 1954. The composers first foray into scoring an actual motion picture was in 1965 which was for the comedy *La Bugiarda*, directed by Luigi Comencini and starring Catherine Spaak.

During his career, the composer has written scores for over thirty movies, these have been varied in genre, but the Maestro has always produced original sounding works whatever the subject matter. Surprisingly, he scored just five Euro/Italian westerns, but these were all key works within that genre. *Adios Gringo (1965), Starblack aka Johnny Colt, and 4 Dollars of Revenge* both in (1966) *Dollar in the Teeth* aka *A Stranger in Town* and *El Rojo* both in (1967). Ghiglia had his own style when scoring westerns, the composer relied upon echoing and vibrant percussive elements within these scores and created haunting and simple themes which he fused together with Mexican sounding mariachis. The composer worked steadily throughout the sixties, seventies, and eighties, working on spy thrillers, robbery capers and adventure tales and scored his last movie in 1997, which was the documentary, ***Galeazzo Ciano Una Tragedia.*** During the early part of the 1970's the composer did slow down his involvement with scoring movies and began to concentrate on his own work. Benedetto Ghiglia passed away on July 4th, 2012, aged eighty nine.

RIZ ORTOLANI.

Riz Ortolani was born in Pesaro Italy on September 4th,1931.He began his career as a singer and moved on to doing arrangements for many of his fellow artists at the beginning of the 1950's as the 1960's approached the composer decided that he would concentrate all of his efforts into writing music for motion pictures. One of his first assignments was to be his most successful and certainly his most lucrative. The music for the documentary film ***Mondo Cane (world of dogs)*** co-written with Nino Olivero contained the song "*More*" which proved to be popular and enjoyed worldwide success. It has been confirmed that the song has been performed on seven million occasions since it was originally recorded for the movie score. Ortolani has worked extensively scoring films and television projects, he was highly successful in his native Italy and much in demand by film makers within the country. But Ortolani also gained a reputation for being a composer of worth and talent outside of Italy and Europe and is one of the few Italian composers from the period of the 1960's through to the late 1970's to be offered numerous scoring assignments in Hollywood and England. Ortolani worked on productions such as **The Glory Guys, Anzio, Madron, The McKenzie Break, The Yellow Rolls Royce,** and **Seventh Dawn. The Yellow Rolls Royce** contained the song, "*Forget Domani*" and **Madron** received an Oscar nomination for best original song, "*Till Love Touches your Heart*". like many other Italian composers Ortolani was very active within the genre of the Italian western. He penned the soundtracks for approximately twenty movies within the genre. **Day of Anger, A Reason to live A Reason to Die, The Unholy Four, Beyond the Law** amongst them. However, the composer did come in for some criticism when scoring Italian westerns as many people, critics and soundtrack collectors alike believed his music was not harsh enough for this genre, except for **Day of Anger.** His approach on westerns did not contain the rawness or the savagery that was displayed by other composers who were active within the same genre. Ortolani's scores being thought of as to lush and romantic, however when he wrote the music for the British made western, **The Hunting Party** (1971) the composer produced a fierce sounding score that contained a dramatic electric guitar rift and had at its heart a driving composition that was performed on strings and punctuated by brass, a 45rpm single was released which was an arrangement of the theme. The composer adding an upbeat percussive background and melodic strings for this version. His soundtracks for thrillers and comedies were well received as were his scores to numerous horror movies and Italian Giallo pictures.

Ortolani scored over three hundred motion pictures and has had an illustrious musical career that lasted sixty years, he passed away on January 23rd, 2014.

VASCO VASSIL KOJUCHAROV.

Vasco Vassil Kojucharov worked on several Italian made movies and excelled it seemed within the genre of the Spaghetti western. Although the composer was not Born in Italy he is as far as many are concerned an important Maestro when it comes to discussing Italian made movies and their scores. Born in Sofia Bulgaria, in 1940, the composer not only worked on westerns, but all genres and his score for **Il Plenilunio Delle Vergini** is one that many fans and critics alike hold in high regard. Kojucharov graduated with distinction and honours in conducting and composition from The State Conservatory in Bulgaria. He studied with Khachaturian in Moscow from 1961 to 1963 and then after this re-located to Italy. It was here in Rome that he began to do work for Nino Rota where he worked on many of the composer's film scores as an assistant and occasionally providing orchestrations. It was also whilst working for Rota that he began to compose Ballets, chamber pieces and suites of music. Kojucharov also began to teach and became the founder of The Sinfonias Carlino Alle Quattro Fontane conducting it in many concerts in the Italian capital. Between 1966 and 1969 the composer scored a dozen westerns and began to collaborate with fellow composer Elsio Mancuso under the name of Vasco and Mancuso on several others including **Django Il Bastardo**, which was released on the Beat records label. The sound that he achieved as a composer was in many ways typical of the Spaghetti western genre, although probably not as grandiose as that of Morricone, it still contained fast paced and catchy sounding themes that became firm favourites with connoisseurs of the genre. Kojucharov would use the trumpet solo to great effect and often lace this with strident strings and an array of percussion, he used harpsichord within many of his soundtracks that added much to the overall ambience. His score for **God is my Colt 45** has some remarkably interesting themes, the composer creating a style that although can be identified as being pure Spaghetti western also has to it an individual and original array of instrumentation. Released in 1972, the movie is the work of director Luigi Batzella who was assisted by Joe D' Amato, although a solid film and an entertaining entry into the Spaghetti western genre, it contains a number of scenes from two other westerns directed by Batzella, **Paid in Blood** (1972), and **Anche Per Django Le Carogne Hanno un Prezzo** (1971). Other westerns that Kujucharov penned on his own included, **God will forgive my Gun** (1966), **One by One** (1968), **Sartana the Grave-digger** (1969), **A Bounty killer for Trinity** (1972) and many others. His collaboration with Elsio Mancuso was a fruitful one, and the composing duo wrote the scores for several westerns. Kujucharov at times also conducted scores for other composers, Franco Salina for example on the movie **Churchills Leopards** in 1970. But it was not just westerns that Vasco was involved with, he provided soundtracks for many genres of film, **Killers Gold** (1979), **The Demon of Incest** (1974), among them. The composer died a few years ago, but the specific or exact date is not publicised and was not made known outside of Italy.

ANGELO FRANCESCO LAVAGNINO.

Angelo Francesco Lavagnino was born in Genoa Italy on February 22nd, 1909, he came from a musical family and was attracted to film music from an early age when he heard an orchestra accompany a silent movie. In many film music connoisseurs opinions Lavagnino was one of the Fathers of Italian film music, an innovator and a highly talented and original music-smith he graduated from the Giuseppe Verdi music conservatory in Milan, with a diploma in violin and composition and spent much of his early career working as a musician in orchestras that were performing in the concert halls and opera houses in Italy. Whilst doing this he also began to teach music and it was during this period that Lavagnino decided to start to compose music for film, his first foray into film scoring came in 1947 when he wrote the music for the comedy drama, **Natale Al Campo 119**, which was directed by Pietro Francisci and starred Vittorio de Sica. As the 1950's began Lavagnino become known within Italy as a composer of great talent, producing music of high quality and able to adapt to any genre or style of film. He also continued to teach music at this time and helped other composers come to grips with the technicalities of film scoring, one such composer was Francesco De Masi who he not only tutored but engaged as an assistant for a few years.

The composers first major film scoring assignment came in 1951 when he provided the soundtrack for **Othello** directed by Orson Welles, Lavagnino also scored the actor/directors **Falstaff-Chimes at Midnight** in 1965 and it was probably because of his first collaboration with Welles that the composer began to be offered assignments on bigger budget productions which included non-Italian movies such as Henry Hathaway's action, drama, adventure *Legend of the Lost,* starring John Wayne, Sophia Loren and Rossano Brazzi in 1957. The British made *Gorgo* in 1961 and Italian/American co-production *Esther and the King* for Director Raoul Walsh in 1960. Lavagnino seemed to excel when he wrote music for documentaries and won awards for his work in this area of film. At The Cannes film festival in 1955 he was nominated for the Palme d'Or for his music to *Continente Perduto* and won the special jury prize at the same festival for the score. In the same year he won the silver ribbon award for this score which came from The Italian National Syndicate of Film Journalists. In 1956 his stunning score for *Empire in the Sun* garnered him another nomination from the film journalists and in 1957 he was awarded the silver ribbon from the same organisation for his music to *Vertigine Bianca.* It is said that Lavagnino was Sergio Leone's first choice of composer when the filmmaker was in pre-production on *A Fistful of Dollars*, but the director after much thought engaged a lesser known young composer named Ennio Morricone, because the film's distributor felt that Morricone would be a better choice. One wonders if the music for the Italian western genre would have evolved in a different way or indeed would have been as successful as it was if Lavagnino had scored the first Leone western. I say this because although Lavagnino's music was always highly original it was certainly more classical in its style and sound than Morricone's and often leaned towards a more Americanized or conventional sound as in Dimitri Tiomkin and Max Steiner with some elements of what can now be deemed as being Spaghetti infused passages. After the success of Leone's first western, many directors and filmmakers began to imitate his style, and some turned to Lavagnino who was to create numerous western scores in his own unmistakable style. In the latter part of 1964 and throughout 1965, Lavagnino composed the score for **5000 Dollari Sull'Asso** which was his first foray into the Euro-western Arena, in addition to this he penned the scores to, **The Tramplers, The Man with the Golden Pistol, The Man from Canyon City**, and **Seven Hours of Gunfire, The Specialist,** and others. The composer scored over three hundred movies during his career, which included, **The Colossus of Rhodes, Conspiracy of Hearts, Five Branded Women, The Last Days of Pompeii, The Naked Maja, Venere Imperiale** to name but a few. The composer passed away in Gavi, Italy on August 21st, 1987.

As well as the Maestro's I have included in the biography section, I would like to make mention of the following composers, who also contributed to the Italian western score, these composers did not write as extensively for the Spaghetti western as some, but their scores went to make up the phenomenon that is now considered by many as one of the most influential collection of scores for the cinema. Composers such as Roberto Pregadio, and Robby Poitevin, who scored a few westerns, but also contributed to other works in the genre either orchestrating or conducting for other composers. Also, Charles Dumont who scored one western **The Belle Starr Story** and Pino Donaggio who wrote the music for **The Fight before Christmas** and **Lead Love and Rage.** Plus, the composers listed next.

BERTO PISANO.

Composer Berto Pisano belongs to the size-able list of Italian composers who worked prolifically in film but never attained the recognition that they truly deserved. Composers such as Pisano regularly scored movies that came out of Italy during the 1960's through to the 1980's producing soundtracks of infectious and original sounding music that were often far superior to the films for which they were created. Pisano's style was very much akin to that of his peers and fellow composers, Gianni Marchetti, Stelvio Cipriani and Nico Fidenco, who were also very productive and active during the same period.

The composer utilized a pop orientated or upbeat sounds for many of the movies that he worked on and fusing this style with a more dramatic sound and at times employing seductive, steamy jazz slanted melodies to create scores that not only enhanced and supported the movies well, but also worked on another level and became pieces of music that were entertaining away from the images that they were originally intended to underline. Pisano worked on numerous movie scores and in recent years has become a firm favourite amongst collectors of European film music, finally being appreciated for his originality as a composer and for his ability as an orchestrator and arranger to create haunting and lasting melodies. **Dove Vizetto** for example contains a score that is typical Pisano, upbeat compositions lay the foundation for the work and these rhythmic and haunting themes dominate throughout, in fact when one listens to the soundtrack it is probably true to say it is more like listening to tracks from a compilation of easy listening music rather than a film score. But this does not take anything away from the quality of Pisano's soundtrack, in fact it adds to its already high standard and makes the listening experience a more enjoyable one. The score has a distinct sound to it and is written and orchestrated in a style that is the essence of Italian film music from the period, haunting, entertaining, romantic, lyrical with touches of drama and mystery I think sums up Pisano's music perfectly. Berto Pisano's most noteworthy credits include, *Kill!* (1970), *Strip Nude for your Killer* (1975), *Patrick Still Lives* (1979), *Malabimba* (1979) and *Burial Ground* (1981) The composer collaborated with numerous artists and musicians during his career, Edda Dell Orso, Alessandro Alessandroni and Oscar Valdambrini amongst them. He scored a few westerns but his scores for these are not available apart from *Uno Dopo L'Altro* which he composed with Fred Bongusto, the compact disc was issued by GDM, and the soundtrack is also available on digital platforms.

GIANNI MARCHETTI.

Gianni Marchetti was born in Rome on September 7th, 1933, he was an underrated composer who was active during the 1960's and 1970's, he scored approximately forty feature films. He scored one western, *I Vigliacchi Non Pregano* aka *Cowards Don't Pray* or *A Taste of Vengeance* in 1967. A CAM LP record was released that contained a few selections of Marchetti's music for the movie, and it was partnered by the composers score for *Seven Red Berets* which was a war movie also released in 1967. The entire score for *Cow-*

ards Don't Pray was re-released on Hillside/GDM in 2006. Marchetti worked on a wide variety of movies, drama's, sexploitation films, war, thrillers, and heist stories. In 1968 he scored the African adventure drama *Caccia ai Violenti* aka *One Step to Hell*, which was always thought to be a western score until the early 1980's. The music was issued on a CAM LP and then in 2013 Hillside/GDM released the entire soundtrack onto compact disc, which is now available on digital platforms. His score for *Seven Red Berets* was also re-released onto compact disc by Kronos records. Marchetti like many other Italian composers during this period used Alessandro Allessandroni and his Il Cantori Moderni. Marchetti died in Rome on April 10th, 2012.

GIOACCHINO ANGELO.

Gioacchino Angelo scored three Euro-westerns in the mid-1960s which were all heavily influenced by American Western soundtracks. *The Damned Pistols of Dallas* aka *The Return of Clay Stone, Three Dollars of Lead* (co-composed with Gianni Ferrio) were both released in 1964 and his third foray into western scoring *Colorado Charlie* was in cinemas in 1965. The soundtracks from *The Damned Pistols of Dallas and Three Dollars of Lead* were originally issued on CAM LP's and are ultra rare items now. Both soundtracks were re-issued onto CD and have become quite hard to find in recent years. Although none of the composers scores for these westerns resembled the Italian style of scoring that we recognise today, they are still interesting examples of western soundtracks from Italy and Europe from the early 1960's. Gioacchino Angelo was born on August 9th, 1899, in Palermo, Sicily, Italy. He studied violin with Franco Tufari at the Viuncenzo Bellini Conservatory, the centre of Palermo's musical life and a flamboyant and vibrant gathering of musicians. Franco Tufari was a revered and respected composer and musician who contributed much to the development of chamber music with Trio Siciliano and others. Angelo became a composer of classical music, from the 1940s through to the 1960s, but he also occasionally wrote for film. His main body of work consists of several operas, ballets, symphonies, and a Mass. He also conducted symphonic concerts and recorded for classical labels. Many of his classical recordings are available on digital platforms. Angelo died on October 14th, 1971, in Ostia Lido, Rome, Lazio, Italy.

EGISTO MACCHI.

Macchi was a highly talented composer who although was groundbreaking and innovative only wrote music for a solitary western which was **Bandidos** directed by Massimo Dalamano in 1967. Born in Grosseto, Macchi moved to Rome to study composition, piano, violin and singing with composer and musician Roman Vlad and Hermann Scherchen, among others. It was around this period that he also studied literature and human physiology at La Sapienza University. During the late fifties, he began his collaboration with a group of musicians Franco Evangelisti, Domenico Guaccero and Daniele Paris. Together with Domenico Guaccero, Daniele Paris, and Antonino Titone, he was one of the editors of the magazine Orders, which first appeared in 1959. Macchi helped establish the Association of new consonance in 1960. He held the position of director the association, and the office of President on three occasions in 1980, 1982, and 1989.

In 1967 he joined Franco Evangelisti's Gruppo di Improvvisazione di Nuova Consonanza, which was an Avant Garde improvisation group that also recruited Macchi's close friend and collaborator Ennio Morricone. In 1978, he participated in the Italian commission for the music of UNICEF, together with Luis Bacalov, Franco Evangelisti, Ennio Morricone and Nino Rota.

In the last years of the composer's life, he collaborated with Ennio Morricone to create and promote the 'New Opera'. In November 1991 he completed La Bohème, a transcription for sixteen instruments and four synthesizers, and Morricone similarly adapted Tosca. From 1967, Macchi became absorbed in work for television and film.

His film work included the scores to **Bandidos** (1967), **Gangsters '70** (1968), **The Assassination of Trotsky** (1972), **Black Holiday** (1973), **Mr. Klein** (1976), **Padre Padrone** (1977), **Antonio Gramsci: The Days of Prison** (1977), **Charlotte** (1981), **Menuet** (1982), **The Malady of Love** (1986), **Salome** (1986), and **Havinck** (1987). His score for **Bandidos** is a highly expressive and dramatic work and features a vocal on the title song by Nico Fidenco, its style is a combination of the Italian western sound and a more conventional approach that can be likened to the Hollywood western score. Macchi combining dramatic driving music for strings, brass, and percussion, but also featuring a haunting trumpet solo by Michele Lacarenza throughout, which becomes the foundation of the entire score.

ARMANDO TROVAJOLI.

Composer Armando Trovajoli scored the music for one Italian made western, but it was a score that has stood the test of time and one that defines the sound of the genre. ***Il Lunghi Giorni Della Vendetta*** aka ***The Long Days of Vengeance***, is a classic Spaghetti western score in every sense, soaring trumpet, electric guitar, echoing percussive elements, tense strings, homely harmonica solos, lilting melodies, and racing timpani. All of which combine to create one of the genre's best non-Morricone western soundtracks. Trovajoli was one of the most important composers for Italian cinema working on over two hundred movies in his career. The composer creating haunting scores for motion pictures using melodic and thematic material and experimenting with jazz. He was an accomplished pianist, composer, and conductor. Who created so many lilting and memorable melodies for the silver screen. He passed away on the 28th of February 2013.

FELICE DI STEFANO.

Felice Di Stefano was born in Arpino, Lazio, Italy in 1915. There is very little information available about the composer, although we do know he was the brother of composer Gianfranco Di Stefano. Felice di Stefano was one of the main composers involved with the Italian western. He scored a dozen or more movies and received a credit for another dozen at least. Di Stefano would sometimes write under the alias of Felix Di Stefano and from time to time collaborated with his brother on various compositions. It is a great shame that none of the composers scores for westerns survived, and he is not represented on LP or compact disc, although there were two 45rpm singles released that contained music from **Ramon the Mexican** and **Blood at Sundown**, which are rare and hard to come by. The style that he employed on many of his western scores was typical of the period when music for the genre was developing and evolving. The composer using solo trumpet, mariachi sounds and strong Hispanic sounding lines to create haunting and tuneful works. He died in Rome in 1995.

IVAN VANDOR.

Ivan Vandor was born in the Hungarian city of Pécs on October 13th, 1932, Vandor moved to Rome in Italy six years later with his family. Which is when he began to take violin lessons and then two years later, he also began to study piano. From 1948 to 1954 he played tenor sax with the Roman New Orleans Jazz Band. Later he became a member of the avant-garde groups Musica Elettronica Viva and Gruppo di Improvvisazione di Nuova Consonanza. At the end of the 1950's Vandor studied composition with Maestro Goffredo Petrassi at the Santa Cecilia Conservatory and after three years graduated. It was also in the same year as his graduation 1962, that he became an Italian citizen.

After graduating in ethnomusicology from U.C.L.A. The composer wrote several books and essays about music composition. He scored several films, such as Mino Guerrini's **Omicidio per Appuntamento** (1967), **Nelo Risi's Diary of a Schizophrenic Girl** (1968), and

Michelangelo Antonioni's *The Passenger* (1975). His only western score was for Giulio Questi's *Django Kill* in 1967. He died in Italy on November 15th, 2020.

GIANFRANCO REVERBERI.

Gian Franco Reverberi was born on December 12th, 1934, in Genoa Italy. The composer was known for his focus on writing music for the Italian western. However, he began his career in rock music and is also famous for being one of Italy's first rock music artists. He collaborated with his brother Gian Piero on the song *Last Men Standing* or *Nel Cimitero di Tucson* as it as entitled in Italy from the soundtrack of *Preparati la Bara*! Aka *Django, prepare a Coffin* (1968) which was one of the many unofficial sequels to Sergio Corbucci's *Django*. The music from *Preparati La Bari!* reached a wider audience in 2006 when it was sampled in the Gnarls Barkley's hit Crazy. Both siblings are listed as writers of the song.

Among his other credited film scores are *Soldati e capelloni* (1967), *A Black Veil for Lisa* (1968), *Chimera* (1968), *Viva América!* (1969), *Venus in Furs* (1969), *La Ragazza del Prete* (1970), *Black Magic Rites* (1973). Reverberi died in Genoa on 8 January 2024. He was 89 years of age.

CARLO RUSTICHELLI.

Carlo Rustichelli was born on Christmas eve 1916. Rustichelli was a composer who not only scored Italian movies, but he also had a moderately successful career writing for Hollywood. His career spanned some five decades, beginning in the 1940's and extending to the 1990's. His output was highly prolific, the composer scoring some two hundred and fifty motion pictures. He was also an arranger and penned music for television. Born in Carpi, Emilia-Romagna to a family of music lovers, he gained a diploma in pianoforte at the Conservatorio Giovanni Battista Martini in Bologna, going then to Rome where he studied composition at the famous Santa Cecilia Academy. After world war ll he met filmmaker Federico Fellini, and via his friendship with the director met Pietro Germi for whom he scored **Gioventu Perduta** aka **Lost Youth**. Which was the composers first major film score. The composer and director went onto collaborate on numerous movies during the 1940's and through until the 1960's. During the mid1960's Rustichelli began to score westerns, many of which were conducted by Bruno Nicolai. These included key examples within the genre such as **Buffalo Bill Hero of the Far West** in 1964, **Kill or be Killed** (1966), **God forgives I don't,** (1967), **One Minute to pray, One Second to die** (1968), **I Quattro dell 'Ave Maria-aka-Ace High or Revenge at El Paso** (1968), **La Collina degli stivali-aka-Boot Hill** (1969) and many more. He also wrote the music for **L'uomo, l'orgoglio, la vendetta** or **Man, Pride, and Vengeance** in 1967 which was released as **Mit Django kam der Tod** in Germany as an attempt to cash in on the popularity of the spaghetti western, thus for many years being part of the western collective, but in fact was a romantic tragedy set in 19th century Spain starring Franco Nero and Tina Aumont. In 1972 he wrote the music for Billy Wilder's **Avanti!** As well as his contributions to the Italian western genre Rustichelli also wrote scores for numerous sword and sandal films. He died on November 13th, 2004.

CHAPTER EIGHT.

IL MAESTRO.

The Final Biography is on prolific composer Ennio Morricone. There is very little more I can add to what has already been said about this talented composer who has been compared with Mozart. So, I will just call this last piece of the book Il Maestro.

ENNIO MORRICONE.

On July 6th, 2020, the world lost one of the greatest musical talents of the 20th and 21st Centuries. Maestro Ennio Morricone passed-away peacefully at dawn in a clinic in his beloved city of Rome with his wife Maria at his bedside. Morricone who was ninety one years of age had taken a fall at his home the week before and was hospitalised with a fractured femur. Although we as admirers of this great Maestro knew that this day had to come, as is does to us all, it was still an immense shock when the sad news filtered through from Italy.

I for one have been listening to the music of Ennio Morricone since 1968, **The Good the Bad and The Ugly** being my first experience of his music. As a young boy I could not have imagined the musical delights that lay ahead, the discoveries and the inventive and exquisite music that he would produce, music that would haunt and beguile, amaze and delight. It is without any doubt that it is his western themes that he will be remembered for amongst the wider cinema going public, but we as collectors and fans of Il Maestro, know too well that these inventive western soundtracks went to make up just a small part of this prolific composer's output. As there is far more to this composer of film scores and concert music. His music not only underlined and supported every movie and TV show he worked on, but it caressed them, elevated and enhanced them, gave support, and added atmosphere making them better movies. The composer's ingenuity and pioneering musical skills had the ability to make a lesser movie more palatable and a great movie outstanding. As this is a book about the Italian western, I am focusing upon Morricone's contribution to this genre alone.

We are told there were a few rules when you were given your golden ticket that allowed you to interview the Maestro, you never entered his study, which is where he worked and composed both his classical and cinema music. You also never referred to him as Ennio, (why would you) he was and still will remain Il Maestro, The Master, The Genius. Also, when discussing his film score's, you never referred to the westerns as spaghetti westerns, (a habit we have all become guilty of). *"Spaghetti was a food stuff"* he said, *"And had no relationship to music or westerns"*. Morricone's first western soundtrack was for the 1963 Italian/Spanish co production **Gunfight at Red Sands,** or **Duello Nel Texas** which was directed by Ricardo Blasco under the alias of Richard Blasco. The score was a very simple and one that really did not stand out as being particularly original, it contained a number of Americanised musical clichés, which even included a title song *A Gringo Like Me* performed in a very Frankie Laine style, being more akin to the sound of the Hollywood western scores of the 1950's. With lyrics that included *"KEEP YOUR HAND ON YOUR GUN, DON'T YOU TRUST ANYONE, THERE.S JUST ONE KIND OF MAN YOU CAN TRUST, THAT'S A DEAD MAN"*. However, it was a serviceable work and supported the movie well. When you listen to the score closely there are little glimpses of the sound that he would achieve in later western scores. From 1963 through till 1964 Morricone worked on approx.; fourteen more movies before being offered another western, **Le Pistole Non Discutono** or **Bullets Don't Argue.** The soundtrack also contained a song entitled *"Lonesome Billy"*. I mark it as an important and entertaining work because it came just before *A Fistful of Dollars*, but the sound that the Maestro created for this movie was still Americanised to a degree and was totally different from the raw and sparse sounding soundtrack he would write for Leone's first sagebrush saga. 1964 was a landmark year for Morricone, this was the period when he began to become noticed outside of Italy, mainly because of his music for *A Fistful of Dollars,* but also because of the body of work that he was accumulating in the film music arena. It was also in 1964 that he scored movies and other projects such as the documentary by director Paola Cavara entitled **Il Malamondo** a score that displays the composer's versatility and also his boundless inventive and slightly eccentric style. Originally Sergio Leone had not wanted Morricone to score *A Fistful of Dollars*, he had listened to the composer's music for **Duello Nel Texas** and thought it to be *"Ordinary and bland"*. He was looking for something different, new and fresh. Leone, however, began to work on several ideas with Morricone, one of these was to use the song *"Pastures of Plenty"* which the composer had already recorded with vocalist Peter Tevis and arranged it for the artist when he was at RCA records. But Leone suggested that the composer provide an instrumental arrangement and replace the vocal with a whistler, the rest as we all know is history. In 1965 Morricone went back to the western genre scoring **A Pistol for Ringo** followed by **The Return of Ringo** both directed by Duccio Tessari. These two movies contained wonderfully thematic soundtracks, with the title songs from both becoming favourites of Morricone connoisseurs. *"Angel Face"* being the vocal version of the theme from for the first movie with the vocalist Maurizio Graf returning for its sequel performing the slightly harder edged title number from **The Return of Ringo**. At the time of the film's release the songs were issued as single 45rpm records, with a vibrantly colourful cover. The scores for both Ringo films are highly regarded, with the second film having a more grandiose sound and containing an epic feel within some sections of the music. The songs contained elements of the pop music that Morricone was involved with before concentrating upon film music. When he was an arranger at RCA and worked with a handful of popular Italian artists of the period of the late 1950's through to the early 1960's, such as Gianni Morandi. And this was something he continued to do as well as scoring movies during the 1960's providing memorable musical accompaniments for the likes of Mina and Jimmy Fontana.

It was also in 1965 that Morricone was re-united with Director Sergio Leone on **For a Few Dollars More**. The second film in Leone's first trilogy was more ambitious than the first, and so too was Morricone's score, conducted by Bruno Nicolai because by this time the composer had become so busy he could not direct the orchestra, it had a more developed and even more inventive musical persona. Morricone employing the unique soprano voice of Edda Dell Orso within the score and the distinct whistling of Alessandro Alessandroni.

In 1966, Morricone penned his iconic theme for *The Good the Bad and The Ugly,* but this was not the only western that he scored in that year. It was a busy twelve months for the composer, *Seven Guns for the McGregors, The Big Gundown, Navajo Joe,* and *The Hills Run Red.* The latter I feel is such an underrated work and a score that is at times overlooked by many. Directed by Carlo Lizzani under the alias of Lee W Beaver, *The Hills Run Red* was an Italian western but contained several trademarks, themes and predictabilities that had become synonymous with American produced cowboy films of old. This was also the first western produced by the ever-industrious filmmaker Dino De Laurentis. Lizanni is best known for directing Hollywood heavyweight actor Rod Steiger in *The Last Days of Mussolini* in 1977 a film also scored by Morricone, and for helming a few lesser known Italian movies including the marginally successful western *Requiescant* in 1967. Morricone's score for *The Hills Run Red* is outstanding and although it is not as epic sounding as some of his other work for the genre is a triumph of film scoring which lends its considerable musical weight to the proceedings and ensures that one will not forget this movie easily simply because of the score.

Seven guns for the McGregor's was a rip-roaring swashbuckler of a western, with fights and action galore but very little storyline, it did spawn a sequel which was released in 1967 entitled ***Seven Brides for the McGregor's*** also scored by Morricone. Both movies were shall we say less than worthy of the Maestro, but he fashioned scores that stood out, the first of the two containing a rousing march with vocals performed by Il Cantori Moderni and a fast paced piece "*Sante Fe Express*".

1966 also saw the release of ***La Resa di Conti*** or as many know it ***The Big Gundown,*** this is the most accomplished non-Leone western, and in many opinions Morricone's best western score. It is filled with vibrant and robust thematic material, the composer providing the movie with a strong and memorable theme. Which was performed over the credits by vocalist Christy. Directed by Sergio Sollima it is part of what is looked upon as a trilogy of films, which includes ***The Big Gundown, Corri Uomo Corri***, and ***Faccia a Faccia***. ***The Big Gundown*** was released in cinemas outside of Italy as a B feature and had been edited heavily, the movie was screened alongside the rather awful Dean Martin spy spoof, ***The Wrecking Crew,*** (which had a score by Hugo Montenegro) the version of the film that was screened in the UK was also edited badly and further cut by the British censors, it was not until years later that we could see the full version of the movie when it was finally released onto DVD. Morricone's score positively shines throughout the movie, with the scene where Cuchillo is being hunted being particularly memorable. Morricone's use of choir, Edda del Orso's flawless voice, thundering percussion, animal sounds, and strident strings combine to reach a crescendo of driving brass that performs the score's central theme. The use of shrieks and squeals in the hunt sequence underlined the urgency and the fear of the hunted and the determination of the hunters to find their quarry. The lyrics purveying the desperation of one of the films central characters as he runs from what the audience presume to be the forces of justice. It was also in 1966 that Morricone penned the score for *Navajo Joe*. Directed by Sergio Corbucci and starring Burt Reynolds in the title role, the composer adopting the alias of Leo Nichols. He scored *The Good the Bad and the Ugly,* in the same year which is a triumph of film making. Set in the time of the American Civil war, this is considered the best of the Dollar trilogy. Although the western film was not uppermost on the work schedule of the composer in 1967, he was still in demand for numerous other genres of film. *Dirty Heroes, Grand Slam*, and the *Girl and the General* among them.

To 1968 and the scoring of western movies became a more prominent feature in the composer's workload. He would collaborate with director Sergio Corbucci twice in this year, plus he would score westerns for Petroni, Leone, and French film maker Henri Verneuil. And it is the Verneuil movie I would like to begin with, *Guns for San Sebastian* which although is nearly always classed as a Morricone western score and a film that is within the western genre, was in my opinion more of an adventure or historical period piece which just happened to be set in Mexico. It was also not an Italian production. Based upon the novel *A Wall for San Sebastian* by William Barby Farherty. The cast was impressive with Anthony Quinn, Charles Bronson, Anjanette Comer, Sam Jaffe, and Jaime Fernandez. The musical score is one of Morricone's most accomplished and romantic sounding soundtracks from this period of his career, and was a more developed and inspired work than many of his earlier works, but it is also a very different film from, *A Fistful of Dollars.* The exquisite love theme from the movie is the core of Morricone's soundtrack, this central thematic piece acts as the foundation on which the composer builds the remainder of his work. The gloriously melodic theme becoming a soaring and unique listening experience, with the distinct and flawless vocals of Edda Dell Orso making a powerful but at the same time emotional impact. The score for *Guns for San Sebastian* rivals *Once Upon a Time in the West,* it has the rawness and the savagery of the Italian western sound within it, but also has a poignancy and heartfelt persona that oozes an emotive and affecting quality, which mesmerizes and beguiles. The music excels throughout the film adding depth, atmosphere, and emotion to the proceedings. The action cues from the score are more akin to the composer's sound and style on *Navajo Joe* with dark and dramatic piano forming the foundation of many cues on which the composer constructs jagged and commanding compositions that are a collaboration of brass and strings, with urgent and shrill woodwinds adding to the atmosphere. There are also similarities to the *Navajo Joe* score, in the tracks that underscore the Yaqui Indians in the film. As well as the unique voice of Edda Dell Orso, there are commanding performances from Gianna Spagnolo and excellent choral work performed by Il Cantori Moderni, this is classic Morricone.

The two movies that Morricone scored for Corbucci in the same year were *The Grand Silence* and *A Professional Gun,* both excellent examples of the Italian produced western. ***The Grand Silence*** is one of the great Italian westerns, everything about the movie is polished. Unlike so many other Italian westerns this French Italian co-production was filmed in Italy in the Dolomites and not in Spain, it is set in a snow-covered landscape rather than an arid and dusty one or the mud laden location as in Corbucci's earlier movie ***Django***. The cast is led by French actor Jean Louise Trintignant who plays the part of mute gunfighter named Silence. The movie also starred Klaus Kinski who as always was excellent as the villain Loco the leader of a band of bounty hunters. The love interest was provided by Vonetta McGee who made her debut in the movie. Plus, there were some familiar faces in the form of Frank Wolff, Luigi Pistilli and Mario Brega. Trintignant's character is pitted against Loco and his killers as he defends a group of outlaws who are hiding out in the hills and a vengeful widow played convincingly by McGee.

The musical score is outstanding, Morricone applying a soft and highly themeatic approach at times. Again we have the scenario where a softer sounding soundtrack makes the moments of violence and action even more shocking and affective. The composer's opening credit's theme in-particular is soothing and calming. *"Restless"* as it is entitled accompanies Trintignant's character as we see him riding through the snow-covered landscape with the credits appearing on screen. Strings, Choir, and percussion combine to create a haunting melody that is given various outings throughout the movie in differing arrangements. Alessandroni also performs Sitar within the score, which is an unusual instrument to use on a western soundtrack, but this is the inventive genius of Morricone we are dealing with, Sitar, harp, and choir combine at times to create stunning fragments of themes that are a delight.

The score for **A Professional** by Ennio Morricone and Bruno Nicolai opens with a pulsating and highly infectious composition that is introduced by discordant sounding brass flourishes supported and interspersed by shouts and shrill whistles, punctuated by percussion and harshly strummed guitar. This introduction builds to a crescendo and gains momentum as it segues into full on, fast paced and aggressive piece which is a background to flyaway strings that purvey a sound that is full of patriotic ferber with Mexican sounding choir embellishing and carrying the composition along. The cue entitled *"Bamaba Viavace"* is an energetic and highly charged piece that is a perfect opener for the score and sets the scene for what is to follow. **A Professional Gun** contains a collection of themes, which relate to the main characters within the movie, there is a clear and effective use of the leit-motif style of scoring which Morricone utilized within many of his soundtracks for Italian westerns. Alessandroni's distinct descending whistle motif is the core feature of the score, accompanying Franco Nero's character in the movie. As well as the central thematic material for the main characters the score contains a sprinkling of fiesta or Mexican mariachi flavoured cues with a Viennese style waltz making an appearance in *"Fiesta"* (Valzer) which acts as the background music for the wedding of Paco and Columba (Giovanna Ralli). The score ends with the grand sounding piece *"L'Arena"* which is heard during the final showdown set in a bull ring, and combines most of the scores core themes. Another western that was produced in this year was **Skyful of Stars** *for a Roof,* directed by Giulio Petroni, it starred Giuliano Gemma and Mario Adorf. Morricone's score reflects the savagery and relentless pursuit of a band of killers, who are trailing the heroes of the movie. But the composer creates elements of melancholy and comedy which accompanies the two central characters. The work employs banjo and whistling alongside choral work, that at times are interrupted by raw, scratchy, and strident strings that are punctuated by brass and percussion. It is a score that although known by Morricone followers is one that at times does slip under the radar and is not discussed enough.

1968 was also the year that Sergio Leone unveiled his Masterpiece, **Once Upon a Time in the West,** the most ambitious film that Leone had been involved with thus far in his career. Morricone created a score that is masterful and mesmeric. Often referred to as Leone's opera where the arias were stared and not sung. This is a more polished and classier type of Italian western, the cast being top-notch, with Claudia Cardinale, Henry Fonda, Charles Bronson, and Jason Robards. It is true to say that Morricone played a massive part in helping to bring this project to the screen in the way that the director had intended with a score that was soaring, eloquent but also savage and dramatic. The music played an even greater integral role than the Morricone/Leone partnership had called for before and went way beyond the integration of the chiming watch theme in **For A Few Dollars More.** The harmonica theme was vital to the movies storyline and accompanied the mysterious character of harmonica throughout the movie. The story included several flashbacks, which by the end of the film all became clear to the watching audience.

Actor Henry Fonda said that Leone cast him in the role of the villain Frank because he was an actor who normally had portrayed the good guy in his movies, and the director knew that the sight of Fonda in a long duster coat and two days face stubble would completely throw the audience adding greater impact to the scene where a family is massacred. This is classic Morricone, and a film and score that saw the Italian western come of age and start to be taken more seriously than before.

After the success of the **Once Upon a Time in the West**, Morricone became even more in demand from film makers, in 1969 he scored twenty-three movies, however just two of these were westerns. **Tepepa**, directed by Giulio Petroni and **The Five Man Army** which although an Italian production was directed by Don Taylor. The latter starred Peter Graves and Bud Spencer and is still looked upon as a weak addition to the genre, many referring to it as a Western version of Mission Impossible, which was a reference to Graves appearance and his less than noteworthy portrayal of the Dutchman in the production. Morricone's score certainly did not disappoint, the opening theme itself being text-book Italian western music if there is such a thing. Guitar, woodwind, shrieks, squeals, and whistles fill the piece as it gradually builds and leads to its martial and vibrant thematic crescendo. The score contained a handful of key themes as in "*Muerte Donde Vas*"? Which accompanied the Mexican revolutionaries with its proud and patriotic sound. One of the most impressive cues on the score is "*The Running of the Japanese*", which accompanies the running of the Samurai character in the movie as he attempts to catch up with the train that he has fallen from. Wild percussive elements are the basis of the cue, Morricone adding to the tension and urgency via strings and brass. *Tepepa*, starred Tomas Milian in the title role and featured a very small contribution from actor Orson Welles, who only took the job because he needed the fee to fund a new film he was intending to make. Set in the days after the Mexican revolution, the film is another of the sub-genre of the Zapata westerns. As with all his western projects the Maestro produced a score that not only supported the action on screen but also yielded an entertaining set of themes and a powerful song which was performed by Christy.

The 1970's dawned and as a composer of film scores Morricone showed no sign of relenting, working on twenty projects for both film and TV in 1970. It was in this year that the composer fashioned a new theme for the established American TV series *"The Virginian"* the series already had an established and popular theme by Percy Faith, however in season nine of the series, producers engaged Morricone to provide a new theme, which was entitled *"The Men from Shiloh"*. It was also in 1970 that Morricone would score an American produced western. *"Two Mules for Sister"*, starred Clint Eastwood and Shirley McClaine, and was directed by Don Siegal. The soundtrack was released on LP record on the MCA label, but this was a re-recording and not taken from the actual film score, which was something that happened a lot with soundtracks during this period. The movie, which was produced by Martin Rakin, was seen as an attempt to cash in on Clint Eastwood's successes in the Leone westerns, which had previously been hinted at in the second rate *"Hang em High"* directed by Ted Post. The full score for *"Two*

Mules for Sister Sara" has since been issued onto CD by American soundtrack label La La Land Records. The composer also wrote the score for **Companeros** in this year, which was another collaboration with director Sergio Corbucci. The score was based on two themes for the central characters with Morricone at times creating parodies of his past scoring styles for. This was especially prominent within the theme **Vamos a Matar Companeros.** Il Cantori Moderni vocalising and Alessandroni whistling adding a scream or shriek and performing guitar, the composer adding little nuances and quirks of orchestration that can only be the sound and style of Il Maestro.

1971 was an incredibly industrious year for the composer, he scored twenty-three movies, but only one western, which was Sergio Leone's **Giu La Testa** or **A Fistful of Dynamite** aka **Duck you Sucker**.

Morricone's score again comprises of a collection of themes for the films central characters, with whistling being utilised once again, and Edda Dell Orso providing an exquisite aural experience throughout. By 1971 the production of the Italian western had begun to slow significantly in 1972 Morricone worked on just three out of a total of thirty scoring assignments in that year, **What am I doing in the Middle of a Revolution, Sonny and Jed**, and **Life's tough that's Providence.** The first two titles directed by Sergio Corbucci, with the third being the work of film maker Giulio Petroni. The sound employed by Morricone on these three examples of the Italian western had slightly altered to what we were accustomed to, as in they were not as raw or inventive, the genre was losing favour outside of Italy probably because of the emergence of more gritty and contemporary set films such as *The French Connection, Shaft*, and the *Dirty Harry* films. Cinema and the tastes of cinema audiences were changing so the appeal of the Italian made western began to decline. Italian filmmakers themselves turning to cop movies or tales of horror. The seventies were also the time of films having song scores, where a music supervisor tagged vocal performances onto the soundtrack of the film in the hope that these would appeal to audiences who would in turn go out and buy the soundtrack album. From 1972 through to 1976 Morricone worked on a staggering seventy-four movies, but during this period would score just five westerns including the three titles I have already mentioned, the composer also scored *They Call me Nobody* and *The Genius*. After which he did not return to the genre until 1981 with *Occhio Alla Penna* or *Buddy Goes West*, a comedy western directed by Michele Lupo and starring Bud Spencer with former boxer Joe Bugner in a minor role. After this Morricone never wrote an original western score until 2015 when he scored *The Hateful Eight* for Quentin Tarantino, for which he won the Oscar. The demise of the Italian western was a great shame as it had indeed raised awareness and interest in the western genre.

But let us not forget that the style of the Italian western which was intended to parody or in effect improve on what Hollywood had previously produced, would also influence the Hollywood produced westerns that followed in the wake of the Italian productions and were also films that were being produced at the same time as the Italian Western was at its height of popularity. Films such as *100 Rifles, Take a Hard Ride, Bandolero, El Condor, Big Jake, Blue,* and ***The Wild Bunch*** to mention but a few. Many bore signs of influences that could only be taken from Italian produced westerns.

Morricone's music too played a massive part in influencing composers that would work on westerns and even in non-western movies, the innovative sounds and groundbreaking style of the composer can be heard. One example of the Morricone influence in a film that was not a western is ***Kellys Heroes***. The scene where Clint Eastwood, Telly Savalas and Donald Sutherland walk down a village street towards a Tiger tank, is scored in the style of Morricone or the Italian western, with shrieks, screams, and racing timpani accompanying an electric guitar solo, as soon as the sequence begins and the audience hear the music they know straight away that the composer is mimicking Morricone, and also the director of the film is paying homage to the Italian western film. There is no doubt that along with Sergio Leone, Ennio Morricone, transformed the western genre in appearance and in sound. This violent, savage and quirky collection of movies gave us a whole new outlook on the stories of the old west and gifted us ingenious and entertaining soundtracks, and more importantly brought to the public's attention a Maestro the like of which we will never see again.

Afterword by Lionel Woodman.

I have just read this wonderful manuscript which gives a personal insight into the Italian composers of the 60's and 70's. It contains unique personal interviews conducted over twenty five years by the writer John Mansell. Many of these composers are no longer with us so this is a great tribute and memory to them all.

Lionel Woodman. Soundtrack Producer Hillside CD production.